REA

a
commitment
to
critical
thinking

ABOUT THE AUTHOR

Carl B. Smith, Professor of Education at Indiana University, is also the Director of the ERIC Clearinghouse for Reading and Communication Skills, the Director of the Family Literacy Center, and senior author of the Macmillan Reading Program. A former classroom teacher and reading specialist, he has written more than twenty books and one hundred articles. His research focuses on children's writing and on curriculum development.

a
commitment
to
critical
thinking

Carl B. Smith

Revised and expanded edition

GRAYSON BERNARD
PUBLISHERS

Acknowledgments

With many thanks—to Zhang Hong for his research assistance, to Kathleen McConahay for giving this book an open and friendly design, and to Susan Yerolemou for adding classroom activities and for her astute editing.

First printing 1990, published by Macmillan/McGraw-Hill Publishing Company
Second printing 1991, published by Grayson Bernard Publishers
Third printing 1991, revised and expanded
Fourth printing 1991
Printed in the United States of America

Publisher's Cataloging in Publication
(Prepared by Quality Books Inc.)

Smith, Carl Bernard.
    A commitment to critical thinking / Carl B. Smith. -- Rev. ed. --

    p. cm
    Includes bibliographical references.
    ISBN 0-9628556-0-X

    1. Critical thinking--Study and teaching.   2. Reading.   I. Title.

LB1590.3   371.3   91-71319
                                              QB191-346

Grayson Bernard Publishers
223 S. Pete Ellis Drive, Suite 12
Bloomington, Indiana 47408

Preface

how to use this book

Our understanding of critical thinking and critical reading changes as our theories change. When we thought critical thinking was analogous to problem solving, we encouraged problem solving in our classrooms. When we thought critical thinking could be categorized into a set of logical skills, we engaged in cause and effect activities and other exercises that raised our sights above the mere retrieving of information. When we thought that we could not distinguish critical thinking from other thinking, we simply read books and discussed them.

More recently we have restated our belief in the need to teach critical thinking and to develop in our students an attitude that challenges ideas and values, an attitude that is essential to thinking critically. In other words we need to define critical thinking and commit ourselves to thinking critically.

This book reviews definitions and helps you in a personal review of critical thinking. It gives you ways to challenge your students chapter by chapter. As you decide how you want to approach critical reading you may want to try the ideas in each chapter to see which ones work best for your students.

This book could give focus to inservice discussions where you and your colleagues test ideas against your collective experiences. As you share new and old ideas, you refine your concepts and are likely to re-read critically.

There are two major resources in the second half of this book. There are numerous critical thinking/reading activities for classroom use. There is also a section of annotations for additional practice and for personal development. The activities are clearly labeled and designed for classroom or tutoring use. Please decide which are appropriate and adapt for your use. The annotated bibliography includes recent conference papers and journal articles. The annotations alone give you ideas you can use even before you decide whether or not you want to pursue the whole article.

Whether you are refining your own definition or are looking for critical reading resources, we encourage you to send us your ideas for improving critical thinking in the classroom.

CBS
Bloomington, 1991

table
of
contents

Chapter 1

critical thinking and reading

Some people think that if you read, you are thinking critically. They feel that the process of comprehending is so complex that higher level thinking has to take place or there is no comprehension. Reading and critical thinking are indistinguishable, according to this point of view.

At the same time that some academics equate critical thinking with all reading, American employers are complaining that they can no longer find employees who think critically. Even those who can read, they say, do not have the training to solve problems and to evaluate alternatives. Since these contradictory definitions are made on the same planet in the same year, it seems clear that the term *critical thinking* has diverse meanings. It might be more accurate to say that there are diverse philosophies at work in those different uses of the term *critical thinking*.

When managers of large U.S. firms bemoan the lack of critical thinking in today's labor pool, and when they point an accusing finger at the schools for not providing appropriate training, they obviously believe that critical thinking is a skill that can be developed and measured in school. They have assessed the skills of their workers and found them lacking. Some current theorists believe that reading and thinking are part of a whole cloth that cannot be cut into pieces, some labeled literal thinking, some labeled critical thinking. Reading is reading; thinking is thinking, they say. The only thing that may set critical thinking apart from other thinking is an attitude of skepticism. (Harste, 1989; Siegel and Carey, 1989)

Where does this leave the classroom teacher? Does the teacher have a responsibility to develop critical thinking? It would certainly seem so because almost every school curriculum lists critical thinking and critical reading as a major performance goal. Curriculum committees, therefore, have decided that critical reading should be taught and measured. Thus most reading tests have a category called critical reading. They assume, then, that the teacher can develop and can demonstrate progress in critical reading as part of a public record.

As can be inferred from the above, the definition of critical thinking, its development in the classroom, and its assessment raise knotty issues for schools and teachers. This book discusses some of the practical issues that teachers face and summarizes some of the philosophical and psychological questions related to the teaching of critical thinking. Our primary concern here is to help teachers define critical thinking/reading and to unfold opportunities and strategies for critical reading. Teachers can then decide how to engage their students in the daily exercise of critical reading. First, however, teachers will have to choose their own definition of critical thinking and then make a commitment to implement it in the classroom.

Critical Is Not Negative

Once I asked a student to give his critical reaction to an article the class had read, and he said: "I don't want to criticize it. I like it." His response reflects a fairly commonsense notion that critical thinking means bad-mouthing the ideas or the writing. As a matter of fact, he had already begun a critical response when he said he liked the piece. By adding his reasons for that positive impression, he would have given his classmates an example of critical thinking. He had decided that the article had some value for him—either a valuable concept or a pleasing manner of expression.

Even those who want to make critical thinking almost indistinguishable from other thinking define critical thinking in words that carry a negative connotation. They refer to critical thinking as representing a skeptical attitude or a cynical curiosity—terms that suggest a search for fraud, lies, and other false representations of the world. (Siegel and Carey, 1989) Perhaps a more appropriate question to ask is: "Does this match my sense of reality?" That question allows both positive and negative reactions. It still allows the reader to search the text with curiosity without predetermining that the response will be negative.

The disposition to raise questions seems to be part of everyone's definition of critical thinking. Whether or not the questions reflect a general curiosity or a cynical curiosity, all theorists see the need for the mind to challenge ideas regularly and to examine their match with the reality of the reader. Norris (1985) pushes the idea further by saying that the reader also must have the disposition to be productive, that is, to give an overt response to the questions that the reader raises about the text. In the most general sense, then, teachers promote critical reading when they encourage students to raise questions about their reading and to answer their own questions. The most general questions being: "Is this text valuable for me?" "Does it match my sense of the world?" By regularly asking students to respond to questions like that the teacher promotes an attitude or a disposition to think critically.

More Precise Definitions

If we are thinking critically about this discussion, we have to ask ourselves whether or not the broad notion of critical thinking as employing a curious attitude works for us. Does it give us enough direction to guide our students? Will we know when our students are making progress? If they seem confused by the general question: "Is this valuable?" will we have enough guidance to help them get off dead center? Can we turn that curious attitude into a public record to show students and parents that we are responsible agents of the community and are teaching or promoting critical thinking?

There are many ways to add more precision to our definition if we so desire. Each step towards precision makes it easier for us to assess progress, but carries the corresponding danger that we will focus only on highly specific behaviors and cut off the flexibility of broad curiosity about truth. Teachers need to decide what level of specificity works for them and their students.

One step towards a more manageable definition is to bring student thinking to a decision point. They have to decide what to do or what to believe. (Norris, 1985) To make those decisions, readers have to weigh alternatives and apply some standards to arrive at their decisions. For example among the five books on the theme of courage, which one delivers the action and the sense of history I want for this project? A teacher may not want to examine the alternatives in public, but the fact that a decision was made forces the mind to evaluate by some process, the importance of the ideas or events in the article.

Even though the terminology and skills involved in reading critically may be somewhat elusive, the development of critical readers has come to be an undeniably important goal of the school curriculum. The rapidly increasing volume of printed material to be read, assimilated, and evaluated, plus the constant propaganda that pounds our senses, makes the ability to read critically a workaday tool and weapon. We use the term *propaganda* to mean one-sided advocacy of a particular idea or belief. From morning newspaper editorials to the commercials we watch on evening television, each day forces us to read and react critically to the obvious and to the obscure.

For example, readers will recognize the different approaches to a school tax hike taken by the chamber of commerce and the local teachers' association; they will note inconsistencies between the headline and text in a movie magazine; they will question the advertisement that promises a bright future for the user of a certain toothpaste or cleansing cream. It is imperative that informed consumers and citizens read with care and that teachers are alert to daily opportunities to apply critical reading skills. The teacher must work toward situations that give pupils a chance to consider purposes for reading other than simple recall. Students then learn to analyze, to draw inferences, and to make judgments on the basis of some standards.

What Is Critical Reading?

A Philosophy of Critical Reading

In this day when teachers are exercising more and more control over the curriculum in their classrooms, they are faced with the problem of defining terms rather than simply carrying out directions. Unless teachers merely replace the directions in a textbook with directions coming from an educational guru, they have to define what they mean by critical reading and develop a set of beliefs or develop a philosophy about how best to conduct critical reading/thinking in their classrooms. Simply asking higher level questions now and then or setting up cooperative groups now and then will not develop critical thinking. If critical thinking is important, teachers have to make a commitment to promoting critical thinking on a continuing basis.

The first step in making a commitment to critical thinking is to establish a definition that is manageable. One of the reasons the Norris definition is attractive for teachers is that it is direct and seems quite manageable—*critical thinking is deciding rationally what to do or what to believe.*

In classroom discussion, therefore, that definition enables the teacher to lead children to the point where they will decide:

- What would you do in that situation?
- What will you do with that information in your life?
- Do you believe the value that was presented in that story?
- What does this information do to your belief system?

A simple definition, of course, does not by itself create an atmosphere of critical reading. In the Norris definition there is the nagging word *rationally.* Alternatives have to be weighed, standards or criteria need to be applied, then a judgment can be made that indicates the action or belief that the reader will adopt.

Norris also suggests that critical thinking will occur in the classroom only when there is a commitment to reach below the surface and then to be productive with your decision. What is implied is that both personal reflection and some kind of public display are part of critical thinking. Once again we return to the interaction between private work and community work. In private we reflect and make one set of decisions, but what sharpens our critical skills is the sharing of them with others. It is probably in this sense that proponents of cooperative learning claim that critical thinking is central to the group process. It is in the fire of group discussion that the mettle of our ideas are refined and hardened.

Robinson (1964) states that critical reading is the ability to apply relevant criteria in evaluating a selection. It is the judgment of the "veracity, validity, and worth of what is read, based on criteria or standards developed through previous experience."

Russell (1956) suggests four conditions essential for critical reading:

1. a knowledge of the field in which the reading is being done
2. an attitude of questioning and suspended judgment
3. some application of the methods of logical analysis or scientific inquiry
4. taking action in light of the analysis or reasoning.

Children who can underline key words and phrases in a selection, who can strike out irrelevant sentences in a presentation, or who can select appropriate titles for stories are all involved in analysis. Skill in analytical interpretation requires practice guided by the teacher and practical illustrations.

Neither teachers nor their students will meet all these conditions at all times. Neither adults nor children can possibly be armed with background knowledge in every field in which they must read. Today's world is too big and human knowledge is too vast. It is necessary, therefore, to equip students with an attitude of general awareness so that they can detect unsupported statements, sweeping generalizations, and conclusions that have been drawn haphazardly. An attitude of suspended judgment may not always be possible. Earlier biases and prejudices affect one's ability to read critically at a later period, as do such factors as age, sex, home background, and sociopolitical attitudes.

As part of his training a student should be taught to recognize his biases and deal with them as a factor in the way he reacts to the printed or spoken word.

The teacher fosters an attitude of inquiry when he teaches the techniques of critical reading. Against such a background children will develop high standards for judging what they read.

One task of the critical reader is to interpret the writer's message, a process sometimes described as "reading between the lines." This interpretation involves an attempt on the part of the reader to understand the logical unity of presentation from the printed material. At this point the reader begins to manipulate the author's ideas mentally in order to perceive relationships and visualize the structure of the selection. The reader asks: "What is the author's main thesis?" "How are the main points supported by detail?" "How do major points within the selection relate?" "Has significant information been overlooked?" The process involves the reader in forming a mental outline, weighing points for their relation and strength, among other things.

Inference

Inference is an attempt on the part of the reader to understand what the author has left unsaid or what he attempts to say without words. An interpolating process, it involves deductive leaps from what is literally stated to what is actually intended: "This is what the author has said, but what does he actually mean?" An example of this type of reading is found in Marc Anthony's funeral oration in Shakespeare's *Julius Caesar*. Marc Anthony continually repeats the phrase: "But Brutus is an honorable man," while he implies the opposite—an effective strategy.

Inferential interpretations depend on a reader's background and intuition. The reader must put several clues together in order to predict possible occurrences or behaviors. He must become adept at using context as a sounding board against which inferences can be tested. And he may need more information about the author: Is the author a satirist? Does he try to manipulate his reader? The reader is involved in bridging the gaps in an author's presentation; he gathers clues as a springboard and then makes the inferential leap. Children make inferences daily by watching faces, tone of voice, and body language. When a reading lesson begins with the teacher telling everyone to hurry and sit still while he has a pinched, intense look on his face, children know that this may not be a relaxed encounter. As teachers we can encourage children to look for similar clues in print and to interpret them accordingly.

Evaluation

How valuable are the ideas we read? The reader is called upon to make judgments as to the worth of the message. Evaluation depends upon the reader's ability to appraise the truthfulness, validity, and accuracy of the material especially as it affects his own life. The first step in evaluation is a reality check—Does this match what I know or believe? The reader may also attempt to determine the accuracy of presentation, the author's professional competence, and the relevancy of his thoughts.

Students who are asked to make judgments may need the aid of *external criteria*, or other references and sources. A pupil with no previous experience with a subject should suspend judgment until he can establish a frame of reference through the use of valid outside sources. *Internal standards* may be all that are required by the student with a strong basis of experience in the area. Difficulty may occur when a pupil's internal criteria, the product of his culture, are strongly in conflict with the prevailing outside sources. Because of an emotional reaction the reader may not be able to suspend judgment until a good deal of evidence is presented on a subject. For example, a Quaker reading a plea to expand the offensive power of the military is influenced by his beliefs to reject this argument regardless of its logic or rhetoric.

The teacher aids the student in clarifying the assumptions he brings to the reading task, in analyzing and ascertaining the assumptions of the author, and in broadening the informational background out of which more unbiased standards of judgment may come. Through discussions, through questions and through thinking aloud, the teacher helps the student appreciate what critical thinking looks like in action.

Judging the worth of a poem or prose selection is another aspect of critical reading. We often call this literary appreciation because it is treated in courses on literary criticism. It is actually a kind of critical reading, using criteria arising from the literary form and from the nature of the experience being described. Literary criticism is different from the reader response theory currently advocated as a means for making text more meaningful to the reader. This theory assumes that the reader is stimulated by the text but creates his own meaning as he continues to respond to the ideas in the text. In this sense the reader is not evaluating the author's text but is building a meaningful text in his own image. What happens in the mind of the reader, therefore, is the important event, not the external text. (Rosenblatt, 1976)

The Art of Questioning

When a teacher asks questions to determine a child's grasp of content, he not only gives the student a type of problem but also leads him to ask questions of his own.

Consider the following selection from a children's book. Formulate three questions a teacher might ask a second-grade child concerning this story:

Susan and Billy watched Billy's new airplane sail through the air. "Look at it go, Susan!" Billy called. "It's as fast as lightning." "Let me fly the airplane," begged Susan. "No, you're too little," answered her brother. "Please?" Susan asked again.

Billy handed the airplane to his sister. "Be careful," he warned. Susan raced across the yard. Gaining speed, she threw the plane into the air. It made a sudden turn and dropped to the ground in a nose dive. One of the bright red wings lay beside the plane.

Proposed questions:

1.
2.
3.

If a teacher asked questions such as: "What did Billy say when Susan asked to fly his plane?" or "What color was Billy's airplane?" he asks for a restatement of fact. If he asks questions such as: "How do you think Billy feels toward his sister now?" or "What do you expect Billy to do now?" "What makes you think so?" he asks for an interpretation.

Tapping critical judgment would require questions such as: "Would it have been better had Billy never shared his toy?" or "Could a toy plane fly as fast as lightning?" Questioning can also lead the child to see the application of the story in his own life: "Have you ever had to share with younger brothers and sisters?" "How would you feel about losing a wing from your plane?"

Critical thinking does not happen automatically. Using questions can lead pupils to become better readers by giving them an inquiring attitude or by giving them examples of ways to think that may make their reading more interesting and more fruitful.

Questions for Restatement

As discussed earlier questions asking for restatement of information serve as checks to determine whether concepts are grasped firmly. Such questions are the easiest to formulate. Often they are looked upon as the first step in a series of questions—necessary, but not nearly as deep as children need to have for a rich experience in reading. They are often questions of:

- detail ("Who planted the flowers in the garden?")
- sequence ("What happened after the rain?")
- main idea ("What was the story about?")

Questions for Analysis

Questions for analysis require readers to extend what is actually stated. They must use both subtle and obvious author cues to move beyond the literal presentation. This is a gap-filling process. Interpretations can be checked against what is actually stated:

- In what season of the year might this story have taken place? What makes you think so?
- Why do you suppose these Plains Indians made their homes from buffalo hides rather than from bark or logs?
- Why was Mother eager for the rain to stop?

- How did the author really feel about animals? How could you tell?
- What is the organizational plan of the chapter?

The answers to these questions depend upon reader analysis and inference.

Questions for Evaluation
Children are usually hesitant to question the printed word. They may view the author as an authority figure. Teachers who adhere to one textbook as the ultimate source of knowledge reinforce such an attitude; so do teachers who attempt to avoid controversial issues and debate in their classrooms. A realistic attitude can be fostered through questions that ask children to distinguish fact from opinion, to recognize assumptions, and to judge author competence, for example.

Questions that demand critical judgment from the reader while using internal or external criteria force critical reading. "Was Billy's reaction the best one under the circumstances? Why, or why not?" "How does this author know so much about forest rangers?"

Encouraging Critical Thinking Through Questioning
Questions in the classroom are the mainstay of teachers. A number of studies have shown that children's comprehension improves when their teachers are taught to use an organized pattern of questions. (Falkof and Moss, 1984) But maybe we are training the wrong people.

If the primary agent in improved comprehension is an active learner, perhaps we would see greater growth by training the children to ask their own questions instead of having them wait for the teacher to come up with questions. From what we know about the value of participatory learning, we should spend more time in getting the learner to raise his own questions. That process not only will direct the reader's attention but will also act as a means of tying various ideas together.

After reading an article or a chapter, children should be able to do more than simply summarize what they have read; even though that's an excellent start. After that the student should see if he can ask himself critical thinking questions, for example: "Why do characters act the way they do?" "Are there cause and effect relations that I can explain?" "Is this message valuable enough to recommend it to someone else?" Then he can decide whether he liked the article or not and try to connect its ideas with other articles or other books that he knows.

With examples from the teacher applied to a specific story, the students could then try to generate their own questions for other stories and use the same categories. The following categories may serve most groups:

- Questions that *seek information* that is given in the text.
- Questions that call for a *summary* or for a statement of the overall theme.
- Questions that search for *relationship*—ranging from time relationships to causal relationships.
- Questions that ask for *evaluations*, such as comparisons of the present text with another one that has some similarities.
- Questions that ask "*What if. . .*" and thus challenge the learner to extend beyond the confines of the text as it appears.

Indeed the very process of asking questions that fit these patterns would help students become critical readers, self-stimulated.

The Teacher as a Critical Reader

The teacher serves as an example as well as a director of learning. In the teacher, children expect a mature reader who can guide them towards being a critical reader. A mature reader should be prepared to detect devices designed to influence a less perceptive reader. What kinds of questions might arise from this passage:

> You know that I was born and raised in Austria. Do you know that there are no remedial reading cases in Austrian schools? Do you know that there are no remedial cases in Germany, in France, in Italy, in Norway, in Spain—practically anywhere in the world except in the United States? Do you know that there was no such thing as remedial reading in this country either until about thirty years ago? Do you know that the teaching of

reading never was a problem anywhere in the world until the United States switched to the present method around about 1925? This sounds incredible, but it is true. (Flesch, 1955)

A competent reader might ask: "How is a remedial reader being defined by this author?" "Does the author refer to remedial cases or classes designed to handle such readers?" (Refer to sentence four in the passage.) "What is the cause against which the author is building his case—his purpose for writing?" "What is his professional field of interest, his specialization?" "Where are the supporting facts for his generalizations?"

Although a reader may have no immediate knowledge with which to substantiate or refute this author's statements, the reader could detect some sweeping generalizations and a rather hastily drawn conclusion. Note the last statement: "This sounds incredible, but it is true." The author appears to have foreseen disbelief on the part of his readers and uses rhetoric to validate the argument—"but it is true." The mature reader knows that something is not necessarily true just because someone says it is. Children can be led to a similar type of intelligent inquiry by teachers who are critical readers themselves and who ask questions which encourage evaluation. (Meehan, 1970)

Chapter 2

classroom exercises in critical reading

There are numerous ways to introduce critical thinking into the language arts classroom. Following are some basic critical reading techniques with examples for appropriate use in primary and intermediate classrooms. Further activities are presented later in this book.

Reality versus Fantasy

In the primary grades one of the first critical reading skills the teacher attempts to develop in students is the ability to distinguish reality from fantasy. She is careful neither to discount fantasy nor to dismiss a story as unworthy because it is fanciful. The teacher realizes that tales of fantasy can spark children's imaginations and elicit creative thought. Even first-grade children, however, can learn to distinguish the difference. They become aware of fantasy signals such as "once-upon-a-time" beginnings and of stories incorporating such traditional fantasy motifs as the beautiful princess, the aged king, the triumph of the younger brother or sister, and reliance upon magic powers and objects.

To initiate awareness the teacher may wish to start with isolated statements and have children respond with a "yes" or "no" depending upon previously established criteria as to the truth or falsity of the statements:

- The moon is made of green cheese.
- A dog can fly.
- Apples grow on cherry trees.
- A kitten is smaller than I.
- A boy can run.

By indicating agreement or disagreement the children grow aware of printed statements that do not match reality. Later, they can discuss the fantasy elements within stories with a "could this have happened?" approach.

- Could the prince really have climbed up on Rapunzel's hair? Why, or why not?
- Could a boy be as small as Tom Thumb?
- Could the cabbage leaves actually have grown as large as a barn? How do you know?

Very young children can also detect the difference between fantasy events and those that are plausible or might have happened. Children can be directed to listen to two accounts of an event, one of which is more true to life than the other. Discussion as to which really could have happened can then be encouraged.

The puppy shivered from the cold. No one seemed to notice him on the sidewalk as last-minute shoppers hurried home with arms full of Christmas packages. He huddled against a tall building to avoid being stepped on.

Oliver Puppy shivered from the cold. "O dear," he sighed, "don't any of those people want a puppy to take home? I do *so* want a people." Just then he had an idea. "I'll ask one of them to belong to *me!*"

Children enjoy changing a factual presentation to one of fantasy by incorporating talking animals or magic events or other fantasy elements. As children get older it becomes easier for them to identify specific incidents in fiction that make the story depart from realism. They can also work successfully with tall tales and the writing of humorists to differentiate reality from fantasy when fantasy is presented as truth.

Connotative Power of Words

Awareness of the power of words is a crucial factor in reading critically. Words can comfort, coax, convince, and deceive. A first step toward intelligent and profitable reading results from the reader's ability to scrutinize a passage to determine what reaction the author is attempting to elicit through the use of words that appeal to the emotions, arouse sentiments, evoke sensory images, or incite to action. A competent reader can differentiate between the dictionary definition of a word—its denotation—and the images and implications the word suggests—its connotation.

Consider, for example, your reaction to the word *child*. Apart from the rather stark denotative definition, "offspring," the connotative implication calls to mind either the sum total of your experiences with children or isolated singular responses—perhaps your childhood memories, the children you teach, the dimpled baby across the street, or the freckled Little Leaguer in your family. Your reaction to the word may be positive and pleasant. On the other hand, words such as *death*, *disease*, *poverty*, and *hell* usually evoke an opposite reaction. These are often called loaded words because, whether you react positively or negatively, the author has intended to trigger a stereotyped response within you. Not all words have connotative power, but those that do can wield a tremendous influence on our lives. Becoming aware of the power of connotative language makes for more critical readers of printed words.

The advertiser is aware of connotations as she markets her product, appealing to the vanity, desires, and weaknesses of the public. Editorials that take a decisive stand on a controversial issue are rich with loaded words, which may either flatter the reader, by appealing to her highest virtues, or awaken fear and distrust for an issue that is new or different. Appeals from worthwhile charities make full use of connotative language for good causes. Election times provide an abundance of campaign materials which carry loaded words that seek to win public approval for a cause or a candidate. In descriptive writing words that appeal to the senses, evoke mental images, and provide literary effectiveness and vividness are used extensively.

Primary Activities
Children who can recognize evocative language are better equipped to make rational judgments about what they are reading and to read critically. Exercises in the primary grades can deal with identification of words with strong imagery. A teacher guides the children to spot such imagery through specific direction:

- Find the words that make you able to almost feel the kitten: (*fuzzy, warm, rough, wet tongue*).
- Find words that give clues to how Mrs. Hill's farm may have smelled: (*fresh cut hay, newly painted fence*).

Similarly, children can find examples of words that appeal to sight, sound, and taste. Many words appeal to more than a single sense. Children with limited experiences develop fewer connotations. Those that develop first center around sensory impressions.

The teacher looks for opportunities to build upon a child's storehouse of personal connotations: "Tell me what comes to mind when I say a word." "Describe what you see or think about." (Use words very close to the child such as *home, mother, love,* and so on.)

Intermediate Activities
It is not the teacher's purpose to encourage students to scrupulously examine each word in a selection. Literary words are usually better appreciated as a *gestalt*—the impact of the sum of the parts. Newspapers, ads, and political speeches, however, provide excellent opportunities for working with connotative language in the intermediate grades.

For example, have children underline the loaded words in a

political speech such as this one:

> Long have I been a citizen of our beloved community. I have watched my children grow here. But now I am deeply disturbed. Never have I witnessed a more tragic upheaval than our city has suffered under my opponent, Major Davis. Taxes have skyrocketed, yet children lie awake at night too hungry to sleep. Our once fair city streets are littered and gutted. Graft and corruption have encamped at City Hall. But, my friends, there is hope. Beckoning us is a bright new horizon, involving us all as free Americans who want desperately to stop decay and begin anew. With a dependable team we can aim toward a better tomorrow. Continuing down the same path can lead only to certain civic death.

- Lead children to note generalities, words with fuzzy meanings, and the ways in which words can be used to skirt issues and to embellish empty statements.
- Discuss connotative words in advertising.
- Find words an advertisement includes in order to appeal to the senses:

"Hair that shines like the sun . . . soft and perfect all the time." (*shampoo*)
"With all the sassy flavor, tender garlic, and mild sweet peppers . . . oozing with twenty-three herbs and spices." (*salad dressing*)
"Seeks out and eliminates cooking odor, musty odors, all kinds of household odors—leaves a fresh clean scent, but never a telltale odor of its own." (*air freshener*)

- Discuss some words that advertisers avoid. See if you can determine why some words are chosen rather than others. (For example, "scent" rather than "smell.")
- Try to determine why a particular brand name was selected for a product. (Joy, Thrill, Halo.)
- Find titles of books that have connotative power.

- Think of words that have recently gained a second connotation ("Protest," "Bohemian"). Which of these words have a general connotation (eliciting similar responses in the total populace) as opposed to a personal connotation?
- Write advertisements or editorials incorporating as many loaded words and words with strong imagery as possible.

Fact versus Opinion

Often it becomes the reader's purpose to distinguish statements of fact from statements of opinion. Factual statements are objective and can be verified; that is, measured in some objective fashion. The truth of the statement: "Johnny is seven feet tall" can be determined by any number of observers using a measuring tape. "Johnny is extremely tall" is not verifiable but rests on one's interpretation of the words *tall* or *extremely*, which may or may not coincide with another's viewpoint.

Consider the difference in presentation of facts and opinion in these examples:

- The temperature and rainfall in the equatorial zone make living there an unpleasant experience.
- Alabama was admitted to the Union in 1819.

Perhaps proof of these statements does not lie within our personal experience. It is not difficult to ascertain, however, that the truth or falsity of the second statement may be checked with a reliable encyclopedia. The first statement depends upon personal background, tastes, and temperament. Certainly some native of the area may consider it to be wrong.

This is not to suggest that we cannot air an opinion unless facts are obtainable. Opinions are an important part of life. We depend upon the commentaries of experts and their opinions, which are based upon facts. We expect a senator to interpret economic developments, for example. We expect an editor to editorialize. The mature reader attempts to maintain critical awareness of the issues so that her opinions can be weighed in relation to the opinions of others.

At times, however, facts are a necessity. We demand facts about daily occurrences in straight news reporting, for instance. We demand this same kind of factual presentation from textbooks.

Distinguishing fact from opinion is not always easy—especially when one's experience or background in a subject is weak. Then the reader must make use of outside criteria. When an author is giving an opinion, she often sends out opinion signals. Children can be made aware of these, just as they can be made aware of fantasy signals. Opinion signals include: "it seems to me," "although not necessarily proven," "in my opinion," "as I (we) see it," and so on. These indicate that the author's expert or inexpert opinion follows.

Primary Activities
Children in primary grades can work with fact and opinion at a simple level. If the teacher makes sure that children have internalized criteria for assessing the verifiability of *one* statement, she can teach them to watch for an obvious signal in another.

- A dog is an animal.
- I think dogs should be kept outdoors.

Intermediate Activities
At an intermediate level, isolated statements of fact and opinion may give way to materials taken directly from the content area. Factual statements may be rewritten as opinions, and vice-versa. The teacher should help children to understand the importance of factual presentations in texts. For example, speculate as to how social studies books would reflect different views if written by strong-minded Republicans, Democrats, segregationists, English people, and so on. The teacher can offer statements such as the following and ask students to indicate which are facts (verifiable) and which are opinion:

- Asia is the largest continent.
- Asia is the most beautiful continent.
- Thurgood Marshall became the first black to be appointed to the Supreme Court on June 13, 1967.
- Thurgood Marshall deserved the honor of becoming a Supreme Court Justice.

Judging Author Competence

Teaching children to evaluate the printed word can be extended to guarded acceptance of the author's right to speak as an authority on a topic.

A mature reader notes both the source of a publication and the author's background. Knowing something about an author's professional training and bias makes a reader more or less open to the author's viewpoint.

Primary Activities
Children in primary grades can be asked:

- Is this author writing about something or someone she really knows?
- How can we find out? (Lead students to the jacket flaps of books, to reviews, to the school librarian.)
- Where might we look to check some of these facts? (Encyclopedias and other references.)

Intermediate Activities
Children in intermediate grades can use such references as *Who's Who in America* and *American Men of Science* for biographical data. They can learn to check the card catalog in the library and the *Reader's Guide to Periodical Literature* in order to determine the scope of an author's work. Children in the middle grades may enjoy writing to publishers to obtain information about an author. They may ask about the depth and breadth of an author's reportage.

Children in the intermediate grades can use sources such as the *Junior Book of Authors* (Kunitz and Haycraft) or sections of the *Horn Book*. The school librarian is an additional resource for reference books.

Practical examples of evaluating author background, education, reputation, and professional position can be profitable for middle-graders. For example, when you read two blurbs about authors of science books you find that the first is head of a science department, director of research studies at a university and has worked as consultant on several science textbooks. The second is highly interested in science, has read extensively, and is primarily a children's author. Ask the children:

- Which of the two might have more background for writing a book on leaf identification?
- What is the standard for selecting one author over the other?
- Can you determine whether publishing house publicity writers and the copy on book jackets have any reason to distort author expertness in a field?

This may result in evaluating the source of the author's expertise.

Determining Author Purpose

Determining the intent of the author enables the reader to evaluate her message better. Does the author hope to inform, amuse, convince, or arouse? Does she wish to state facts, deprecate, or dispel doubt? The purpose of an author's work often determines where it is published. If she wants to increase the knowledge in a certain field substantially by reporting her research results she may choose a scholarly journal with limited readership. If she wants to appeal to a wide audience she might choose *Reader's Digest*. Similarly, the *Congressional Record* probably carries a more direct account of a Senate bill you are following than the editorial page of your newspaper. The purpose for which each piece is printed is different.

Children can learn to become aware of how author purpose may slant a presentation. For example, Robert Lawson's delightful book *Ben and Me* is a fictionalized account of the scientific achievements of Benjamin Franklin as "told" by a mouse who takes full credit for Franklin's discoveries. It can be compared with the D'Aulaires' book *Benjamin Franklin*, a biography of this famous inventor. Children can be taught to discern differences in presentation because of differences in purpose.

Stories can be assessed for author purpose. A simple classification scheme such as "fun" or "information" may be a good starting point for beginning such work. Newspapers and varied news accounts may make the point for intermediate-grade students. They may also engage in such activities as:

Reading selected paragraphs with readily determined purposes. For example, one paragraph may inform the children about the new school cafeteria—size, cost, seating capacity, and hours it is open. Another may urge students to take care of the cafeteria, reinforcing the rules while appealing to school spirit.

Writing articles with different purposes. Using the same subject matter, have children write a piece with a specific purpose in mind that is different from other children's pieces. The purpose can be to amuse, to inform, to frighten, and so on. Compare the different articles.

Collect different accounts of the same event. Show those which are presented in straight news style as opposed to feature presentations. Determine the slant of the articles, the author purpose, and the way author purpose can be determined in the article.

Propaganda Techniques

In 1937 the Institute of Propaganda Analysis reported seven techniques whereby unwary readers could fall victim to propaganda. Since then, more than in any other area of critical reading, identifying propaganda has been a standard classroom activity. The original 1937 list of techniques has been expanded, interpreted, and repeatedly redefined by its users. Basically, it consisted of:

1. bad names
2. glad names
3. transfer
4. testimonial
5. plain folks
6. stacking the cards
7. band wagon

Bad names is a method by which readers are encouraged to make a negative judgment about someone or something without examining the evidence cautiously. The writer intends to provoke an emotional reaction through the use of words with unpleasant connotations.

Avoidance behavior is sought by name-calling: "Relieve irritating itching"; "The situation is a rotten-smelling mess."

Glad names is a method that is also dependent on the connotative appeal of words. In this case the propagandist appeals to our senses, our noblest ambitions, our feelings of love and of loyalty. "Lovers of justice," "seekers of truth and honor," "dedicated to democracy," and "delicate demure beauty" are examples of the ways glad names are used to arouse a pleasant response and insure acceptance or approval before the reader scrutinizes the evidence.

Transfer is the utilization of long-standing feelings of admiration for something in an attempt to precipitate the same reaction toward a different product or issue. Politicians cite their church affiliations, hoping for the transfer process. Beauty queens smile beside many different products, and the public desires to emulate the beauty who is selling the product.

Testimonial involves an authority or some well-known person who endorses or rejects some product, service, charity, or issue. The propagandist attempts to play upon the name and fame of the individual in order to convince the public to react in the same way this famous person does. Testimonial is similar to transfer; for example: "Janie Jansen, famous screen star, uses Tress, the shampoo for beautiful women."

Plain folks is the title given to the attempt—often by public speakers such as politicians, ministers, and business people—to gain favor and win confidence by imitating the speech patterns, dress, and interests of those whom they seek to impress. "As a boy on the farm, I watched my Daddy struggle."

Stacking the cards is a method of withholding some element of truth. Omission of truth or slanted judgment may make truth appear to be falsehood and vice-versa; for example: "You know that Roosevelt was betraying us because he made secret deals with Communist boss Stalin."

Band wagon is a follow-the-crowd approach. All are urged to join with the masses and to team with a winner; for example: "More doctors use _____, the number-one selling brand."

A ready source for initial classroom work with propaganda is advertising. Ads are easily obtainable and highly interesting to intermediate-grade pupils. Newspapers and magazines are rich sources of advertisements.

Ability to recognize propaganda is not a sure indicator of the ability to resist it, therefore the teacher strives to give as many concrete examples and applications to actual experiences as possible.

Evaluating the Critical Reader

The child who becomes a critical reader can, in retrospect, judge the veracity, worth, and validity of what she reads. She judges the author's work; she can distinguish reality from fantasy, can determine author purpose and competency, can note instances of evocative language, and can incorporate outside resources in order to check facts. She becomes aware of propaganda and the effect it can have on her life. She can successfully analyze arguments, grouping the points made and evaluating the conclusions. The critical reader makes use of her skill daily in newspaper reading, incidental reading experiences, and in reading for pleasure. She is likely to become a more intelligent voter, citizen, and consumer as a result of her informed skepticism.

Chapter 3

the social
process of
critical
thinking

The activities described in the preceding pages are those that have been used by teachers to lead students to understand the kinds of things that a critical thinker does, that is, gather alternatives, compare, and use some standards to make a decision. If we were to adopt Norris' definition (1985), we would push that decision into the external world. Once an action or a belief has been established, the reader/thinker has to make it public. He has to share it or make it productive in some way. That makes us wonder if the social environment of the classroom makes a difference in the development of critical thinking.

Recently much has been written about learning groups and the advantages of cooperative and collaborative learning. When given a common problem to solve and when assigned specific responsibilities within their group for solving the common problem, children often work through the process and exhibit critical thinking in action. For example, if they have to decide how to change the ending of a story or decide what conclusions could be drawn if some part of the text were changed, or are asked to figure out the values that a character reflected in a story, they explore, argue, and decide among themselves.

This social process of interacting and collaborating to achieve a common purpose has a significant advantage for critical thinking. It forces ideas into a public forum. As is true in most discussions over issues, the cooperative group arrangement supplies alternative points of view and the need to sort out those views. Here the learner cannot be complacent because someone else is there to challenge his perspective. With guidance from the teacher, the students can locate additional information to aid in their decision-making and can realize that a variety of standards may be used to evaluate a point of view. Perhaps something more is needed than to say you heard it on television.

Not all social learning requires critical thinking. When groups get together to help each other to prepare for a test or to identify the important events leading up to the War Between the States, their interactions may be more concerned with how to make each member of the team successful, not how to make some decision about the artistry or cogency of a passage. But even then, the opportunity for making decisions among alternatives and deciding what to believe is enhanced by the interconnections of all these young minds.

It makes it worthwhile, therefore, to look more closely at cooperative learning as a vehicle for critical thinking. Let's examine the definition of cooperative learning, look at the reported effectiveness of cooperative learning groups, and project ways in which cooperative groups can promote critical reading and critical thinking.

What Is Shared Learning?

Shared learning is variously known as cooperative learning, collaborative learning, or other small group learning and it is praised by educational theorists for its influence on critical thinking. As far as instructional goals are concerned, all these group arrangements aim at improving critical thinking. Therefore, for our convenience, we shall call them all "cooperative learning."

Cooperative learning groups set up students in teams; team members are responsible for one another's learning as well as their own. Students encourage and help each other master skills and content that are presented. Students convey to one another the idea that learning is important, valuable, and fun. (Slavin, 1987) According to Slavin, cooperative learning is not an instructional method that can be used from time to time; it is an alternative to the traditional mode of instruction.

Johnson and Johnson (1986), define cooperative learning as a generic classroom learning technique which requires students to work and talk together about academic material while learning effective, positive interpersonal skills. In the cooperative classroom, small groups of students (two to six members) can be seen discussing, explaining, and learning together, regular academic subject material. Students also can be seen practicing effective social skill behaviors in their groups: behaviors which are necessary for working effectively with others, for establishing positive friendships with peers, and for maintaining healthy family relationships. Teachers act as advisors while the groups are working; they are available to help students with the lesson and with social skill behaviors.

Cooperative learning benefits achievement. Johnson and Johnson, (1986) report that in cooperative learning situations more students achieve at higher levels, and they retain the information longer. This increased achievement and retention is true for all ability levels: low, middle, and high. Talking about their school work rather than quietly completing worksheets gives students an opportunity to be more actively involved and more responsible for their own learning. It helps them become critical thinkers. According to Johnson and Johnson, cooperative learning has been shown to facilitate:

- the mastery of concepts and principles
- the application of information to other settings
- problem-solving skills
- creativity
- verbal skills
- the ability to take another person's perspective.

All of these characteristics of course relate to critical thinking.

Chapter 4

research on the effects of cooperative learning

Not surprisingly, the evidence is mounting to show the favorable effects of cooperative grouping. The sample studies presented here indicate that both teacher and students are active participants in operating cooperative groups. The teacher gives focus and organizes essential material, providing overview schemes, questions for various levels of reading, resource books, assignment of student roles, and so on. As the groups carry out their inquiry, the teacher helps keep them moving, clarifies student roles, and asks thought-provoking questions that reflect her own sense of curiosity about the issue under discussion.

The students each contribute the energy and the inquiry required by her role—information gatherer, discussion leader, evaluator, recorder, and so on. Each has a personal report to make and thus produces a description of her work that may be discussed and evaluated as the teacher wishes.

It is easy to understand that a high level of focused energy by the learner is likely to produce favorable results. That energy is sustained by the group dynamics where each member has to keep delivering something to enable the group to be successful. A real sense of community needs to be developed for these groups to function advantageously. If the group's job is to decide what courage means in the life of a third grader and to write a report or a story that demonstrates their concept of courage, each member has to contribute a fair share according to her role. If one member is slow to bring sample stories for the rest to read, all the others will prod her into action. After all, if she shirks her responsibility, they all suffer. An important value is communicated through this shared responsibility.

Once a learning group is formed, that does not eliminate personal work and private learning. Individual work, personal reflection and repetitive practice remain a consistent part of all learning. That may be particularly true for refining those skills that help a person polish her reading, writing, and computation—expanding vocabulary, using figurative language, becoming a fluent reader, learning to punctuate effectively, calculating results through efficient formulae, etc.

Some objectives may not lend themselves to an effective gain through group interaction. Perhaps that explains why many cooperative learning experiments show significant effects for attitude and social skills but not for knowledge and thinking skills. Many knowledge and thinking procedures in language arts seem to require personal attention and persistent practice for fluency and power. Realizing this, the teacher selects problem-solving type projects for cooperative learning groups and personal assignments for those learnings that rely primarily on the private practice of the individual learner.

Effects on Attitude and Achievement

Wheeler and Ryan (1973) reported a study of the effects of *cooperative* and *competitive* classroom environments on the attitudes and achievement of elementary school students in Social Studies. Eighty-eight fifth- and sixth-graders were randomly assigned to one of three treatments: *cooperative, competitive,* or *control*. The two experimental groups were exposed to the same Social Studies content for 18 days and worked on inquiry-related problems within sub-groups (cooperative) or independently (competitive). The control group did not receive the same instructional content. Two attitudinal measures were given to cooperative and competitive subjects (n = 58) as a post-test. All three treatments were given an achievement post-test.

Procedure
Both the cooperative and competitive groups were exposed to the same content—a unit on *adaptation* developed for this investigation. The unit focuses on the Iban (an ethnic group in Borneo) and the Eskimo of northern Alaska. However, the organizational patterns for instruction differed between the *cooperative* and *competitive* groups. Cooperative subjects were randomly assigned to sub-groups of either five or six members apiece. Each sub-group cooperatively worked together to complete various inquiry-type activities in a workbook created by the investigators. Members of the sub-groups submitting the best workbook (as evaluated by the investigators over each five-lesson period) were awarded a "pop" poster as a reward.

Cooperative Learning Format
Within each cooperative sub-group, individual inquiry tasks were further delineated through a division of labor. For example, in one lesson sub-groups were asked to find evidence from slide pictures to support or not support hypotheses generated in a previous lesson. The slides showed scenes that depicted the Iban way of life. The *coordinator* for each sub-group was to keep her sub-group oriented to the task by asking questions such as "Is there any evidence to support this hypothesis?" "Who can list the evidence to support this hypothesis?" and "Who can list the evidence in this picture?"

The *analyzer's* role (in this cooperative learning sub-group) was to determine if the evidence submitted by sub-group members was relevant to the hypothesis under consideration. Thus, if a sub-group member suggested that a bowl of rice found in one of the slide pictures supported the hypothesis that the Iban were a religious people, the analyzer could then ask: "What does the rice have to do with religion?" or, "Is there any other evidence to be found in the slide pictures to make you think that there is a connection between the rice and religion?" After the sub-group had arrived at a group decision as to what evidence should be included to support a particular hypothesis, the *recorder's* task (in this cooperative learning sub-group) was to list the evidence in the sub-group's workbook.

Competitive subjects worked on the same inquiry workbooks, but individually, rather than in sub-groups. After each five-lesson period, posters were awarded to the six individuals with the best workbook.

Control subjects studied a unit of Social Studies content different from the content studied by the two experimental groups and did not engage systematically in inquiry activities.

Results of the Study
Results indicated that *cooperative* subjects, significantly more than the *competitive* subjects, liked Social Studies class, sharing information, working together, talking with one another, and receiving group versus individual grades. However, no significant difference between *cooperative* and *competitive* groups was found on achievement, although both groups were superior to the control group. An analysis of variance was used to analyze the data. Significant F values in favor of *cooperative* over *competitive* were found for main effects due to treatments on all three measures (perception, $F = 244.33$, df = $1/54$, p < .0001; attitude toward social studies instruction, $F = 5.40$, df = $1/54$, p < .05; attitude toward *cooperative* situations; $F = 49.46$, df = $1/54$, p < .0001). Anxiety and interaction effects were non-significant on all three measures.

Four Conditions Studied
In another study Lew, et al. (1986) examined the effects of collaborative learning. The effects of four conditions were investigated: (a) opportunity to interact with classmates, (b) positive goal interdependence, (c) positive goal interdependence with a collaborative-skills group contingency, and (d) positive goal interdependence with both collaborative-skills and academic group contingencies. The dependent variables were achievement, cross-handicap relationships, and voluntary use of collaborative skills. Two populations were studied:

34

(a) eighty-three eighth-grade non-handicapped students and (b) four socially isolated and withdrawn students (two eighth-grade and two eleventh-grade).

Results

The results indicate that positive goal interdependence with both collaborative-skills and academic group contingencies promoted the most positive relationships with non-handicapped classmates, the most frequent engagement in cooperative skills, and the highest achievement.

In sample 1, the achievement results for the three eighth-grade English classes indicate that there were no significant differences among conditions for the tests given during the baseline condition. The baseline condition consisted of assigning vocabulary words on Monday, giving students a non-vocabulary assignment on Tuesday and giving them the choice of working alone or with up to three classmates to complete the assignment, giving students the choice to work alone or with up to three classmates to review the vocabulary words for 20 minutes on Thursday, and giving them the 15-minute test on Friday. All instructions, feedback, and rewards were presented to individuals. No contingent reinforcement was used other than individual grades recorded in the teacher's grade book). However, an overall ANOVA and post hoc contrasts revealed that after the study was completed, the students in the two *cooperative* learning conditions tended to achieve higher than did the students in the individualistic condition, $F(2,77) = 2.32$, $p < .10$, with no significant differences existing between the two *cooperative* conditions. In the English class within which specific contingencies were implemented, students achieved higher in the positive goal interdependence and group contingency treatments than in the baseline treatment, with the highest achievement coming in the combined academic and social skills group contingencies treatment, $F(5,125) = 3.53$, $p < .01$.

In sample 2, the four targeted students achieved higher in the positive goal interdependence and group contingency treatments than in the baseline treatment, with the highest achievement coming in the combined academic and social skills group contingencies treatment, $F(5,15) = 3.25$, $p < .05$. Also, the amount of time the four targeted students spent *withdrawn* and *isolated* from their classmates decreased with the introduction of a collaborative skills group contingency in the vocabulary study time and dropped even more when an academic group contingency was added, $F(5,15) = 3.51$, $p < .05$.

The targeted students made more task statements during the free-choice study time after a collaborative-skills contingency was introduced in the vocabulary study time, with the highest rates of task participation resulting after the combined social skills and academic group contingencies were introduced, $F(5,15) = 3.27$, $p < .05$. Similar results tended to be found for maintenance statements, $F(5,15) = 2.68$, $p < .10$.

Chapter 5

promoting
critical
thinking
in the
classroom

Ericson, et al. (1987) describe three content area reading strategies—Anticipation-Reaction Guides; Text Previews; and Three Level Study Guides—that capitalize on cooperative small group learning and emphasize higher order critical thinking. The need for providing students with more effective strategies for reading and critically commenting on their text assignments led faculty at Sutter Junior High School and English professors at California State University to apply for a California Academic Partnership Program Grant. This school-university partnership in the content areas of English and Social Studies has produced an in-service program based on assumptions integral to content reading. (Ratekin, et al., 1985) The two major assumptions are that (1) teachers need to vary organizational settings and instructional methods and (2) they need to plan activities for developing students' readiness for learning, acquisition of information, and internalization of concepts.

The in-service program introduced content area reading strategies to Social Studies and English teachers in the following format. First, each content reading strategy was demonstrated in Social Studies and English classrooms by the university resource specialists as the classroom teachers observed. After the demonstrations, a seminar was held to discuss the teachers' observations and evaluations. At this time, the teachers and resource specialists noted successful features and possible modifications. Each demonstration was video-taped for the seminars and for later editing and use with other content area teachers.

The Anticipation-Reaction Guide

An anticipation guide is a series of about five teacher-prepared statements related to the topics of a short story, poem, or other selection. Before reading, students agree or disagree with the statements and discuss the reasons for their answers. The statements may also serve as a reaction guide following reading and as topic sentences for a writing assignment. See Figure 1.

The value of the anticipation-reaction guide strategy is based on three premises. First, students need to draw on their background knowledge in order to comprehend what they read—they must integrate new information with old. (Rumelhart, 1984; Smith, 1982) This is precisely what students do in responding to the guide, which as a pre-reading activity encourages students to draw on background knowledge. An anticipation guide reveals something about students' knowledge and beliefs so that teachers can fill in gaps when necessary. In short, the guide helps students link literature with the events of their own lives. Second, comprehension is enhanced when students are interested in a topic. (Baldwin, Peleg-Bruckner, and McClintock, 1985; Belloni and Jongsma, 1978) Third, reading and writing should be integrated. (Boyer, 1983; Stotsky, 1983) Students who write about a selection are often better able to understand it, since they have had to organize their thoughts and are encouraged to think beyond the explicit text.

Figure 1
An Anticipation-Reaction Guide

Caged

Directions: Read each statement below. If you agree, put a check in the "Before reading" blank. If you do not agree, do not put a check in the blank. Directions for the "Author's Ideas" column will be given later.

Before reading		Author's ideas
_____	The creatures in pet stores are happy and contented.	_____
_____	People sometimes commit cruel acts without realizing that they are cruel.	_____
_____	Freedom is more valuable than money.	_____
_____	Unusual behavior sometimes frightens people.	_____
_____	Two people can be a part of the same event yet have totally different understandings of it.	_____

Ericson, et al. (1987) lesson plan to promote critical thinking through cooperative learning in English/Social Studies classes. Based on *Caged*, a short story by Lloyd E. Reeve.

The Text Preview

The Text Preview is an introduction which provides students with a detailed framework for comprehending a selection. It consists of three sections: one to build interest; a synopsis; and a brief review of characters with definitions of key vocabulary and several questions to guide reading. See Figure 2.

**Figure 2
A Text Preview**

Build Interest

Many adults read fairy tales to their children. Did any adult ever read fairy tales to you? Which ones do you remember?

Many fairy tales have a princess who falls in love. The young man she falls in love with must often prove himself worthy to her father, the king. Perhaps he must slay a dragon or survive other dangerous experiences. In some fairy tales, the young man even saves the princess from some horrible beast.

Stories like this are not only for children, however. Stories for teenagers and adults may have many similarities with fairy tales. For example, there are many stories in which modern day parents disapprove of the boy their daughter loves, but they change their minds about him when he does something wonderful, and everything ends happily. Can you think of examples from television or the movies which are modern day fairy tales?

Sometimes in a story or television program something happens that you don't expect. Maybe there is a sad ending instead of a happy ending, or the thief turns out to be a king in disguise. Another unexpected ending might involve having the ugly woman turn out to be a beautiful fashion model working under cover for the police. Can you think of other examples?

Synopsis

In *The Lady or the Tiger*, a king has an unusual way of deciding if a man accused of a crime is guilty or innocent. The accused man is forced to walk into an arena and must open one of two doors. Behind one door is a ferocious tiger who immediately tears the man to pieces as punishment for being guilty. Behind the other door is a beautiful woman who immediately marries him as a reward for his innocence. All the people of the kingdom are required to attend this trial.

Review of Characters, Vocabulary, and Guiding Questions

Now it happens that a common man falls in love with the king's daughter. She loves him in return. But the king finds out about their love and the young man's fate is to be decided in the arena. The princess knows which door hides the tiger and will be able to give her lover a signal. But she is very jealous of the beautiful young woman behind the other door.

What signal does she give her lover? You will have to read to find out.

Before you read the story, we want to tell you again the three most important people in it. They are the king, the princess, and the young man.

There are also some words we would like to define:

The king is "semibarbaric" and "authoritarian." "Semibarbaric" means that he is only half civilized. The other half of the king enjoys bloody shows in the arena. "Authoritarian" means that he demands that everything be done his way.

The princess is "fervent" and "imperious." "Fervent" means that she openly shows her feelings. "Imperious" means that she demands her own way, just as her father does.

As you read, be thinking of these questions:
- What signal does the princess give her lover?
- What does the young man find behind the door he opens?
- Why did the princess choose that door?
- If you were writing this story, how would you have ended it?

Ericson, et al. (1987) Based on *The Lady or the Tiger,* by Frank R. Stockton.

The premises for use of the Text Preview are similar to those for the Anticipation-Reaction Guides. Essentially, it encourages use of background knowledge, particularly in the initial interest building section. To construct Text Previews, a teacher should first develop an interest-building section: several statements and questions which connect the major topics and issues with experiences familiar to students. For the next segment, the teacher writes a synopsis which may describe setting, characters, point of view, tone, key elements of plot (excluding the outcome or resolution), and the theme. In the initial segment, the teacher reviews the main characters, gives definitions of important vocabulary, and poses several questions for guiding students' reading. Previews should be about 400 words long, but the teacher should take into account the ability and age levels of the students. Ericson, et al. (1987) report that students responded to the text preview strategy favorably, saying they were able to understand the story better.

Three Level Guides

Three Level Guides were used to generate discussions on questions and to stimulate students' *critical thinking* during and after reading. See Figure 3. To construct a Three Level Guide, the teacher should analyze a reading selection for major concepts and important details and develop questions that reflect these concepts and details at multiple levels of understanding. Students discuss and defend their answers in small groups and eventually contribute to a large group discussion of each question.

Figure 3
Three level study guide for chapter 20—
The Gathering Storm

Directions: Using your book, *American Spirit,* answer the following questions.
Key vocabulary
1. Secession = (*state withdrawing*)
2. Compromise = (*reach an agreement*)

Level 1: Right there on the page
1. What problem arose when the U.S. gained the lands of the Mexican Cession?
   (*because slavery was back*)
2. Why was Senator Henry Clay's compromise plan of 1850 not liked by everyone?
   (*because the north was gaining too much power*)
3. Who disliked Clay's plan? Why?
   (*Senator John C. Calhoun of South Carolina because the north was gaining too much power*)
4. Who liked Clay's plan? Why?
   (*Senator Daniel Webster of Massachusetts. He believed the union was in danger*)

Level 2: Think and search
5. Why was Clay's compromise of 1850 called "a compromise"?
   (*because he wrote what he thought the people would agree with*)

Level 3: On your own
6. Is slavery still a problem in the world? If so, where, what countries?)
   (*Yes, India*)
7. Is racism still a problem in the world? (If so, where, what countries?)
   (*Yes, Lebanon, Saudi Arabia*)
8. What can we, as a people who value human rights, do about racism?
   (*We can negotiate and encourage friendship between the groups*)

Ericson, et al. (1987) One student's responses to the questions are given in italics in parentheses.

Chapter 6

changing philosophies about critical thinking

A modern attempt to define critical thinking for education received its biggest impetus from John Dewey in the 1930's. His concept of school as exploration or inquiry set the stage for continuing attempts to give teachers and students instructional objectives and strategies to achieve higher order thinking skills or critical thinking. Dewey was interested in what is often referred to as process, not product. School is a place where children explore questions that interest them, thus it is the procedure of learning that is important to Dewey, not what is learned. Since most communities and most curriculum theorists believe that identifiable outcomes are also important for American students, most post-Dewey attempts to define critical thinking and critical reading tended to give it a measurable outcome.

Some theorists, as will be seen later, also believe that critical thinking is intimately linked to specific knowledge. In other words, a person has to possess a substantive body of knowledge in a subject before critical thinking strategies or skills can be applied. That theory stands in opposition to the process-first proponents and to those who would teach critical thinking as a separate entity. Most reading programs do not feel threatened by this theoretical conflict between knowledge and procedure because reading textbooks usually spend time building background and a knowledge base as a foundation for teaching and applying critical thinking.

Attempts to define critical reading in the 50's, 60's, and 70's aimed at establishing a behavioral description that contained enough specificity to measure it and to report reliable results. In the 80's some educators began a movement to counteract the emphasis on behavioristic skills. They called for a return to the process approaches of Dewey wherein the schools'/teachers' role is to create an environment for exploring children's interests. The individual child is the center of their attention, not the community objectives. Reading, writing, and discussing are seen as natural phenomena used to search for meaning. Language modes are all part of one whole cloth and should be viewed holistically instead of as parts that contribute to a whole. Students, they say, do not learn to read, but rather they use language in all its manifestations as a way to explore interesting things, that is concepts or events that interest individual children.

Interdisciplinary Interests

During the 80's, the discussion of critical thinking has become more and more interdisciplinary, and has attracted more scholarly attention. From both theoretical and practical perspectives, scholars and researchers have made enormous efforts to clarify and define the concept of critical thinking. Such efforts are necessary because definitions shape our decisions and policy making in education.

In an essay on critical thinking, Sternberg (1985) identifies three major traditions which theorize about the nature of critical thinking: the philosophical, the psychological, and the educational. Discussion of critical thinking from these three perspectives has contributed to our understanding of the nature of critical thinking and consequently to the improvement of its instruction.

Philosophical Tradition

According to Sternberg, the philosophers' concern for the nature of human thinking can be traced back to their ancient Greek ancestors, such as Plato and Aristotle. In the twentieth century John Dewey founded the modern critical thinking movement. He saw education as a way of thinking and exploring, not as a routine for gaining specific knowledge. To Dewey the process of learning was central, not the outcome. Recently, educational philosophers, Robert Ennis, Richard Paul, and Matthew Lipman have been preoccupied with the theoretical and logical aspects of human thinking. These philosophers primarily engage in the inquiry and explication of the basic elements contained in critical thinking and how it is different from other thinking. To a great extent, they believe that formal logic systems are essential to human thinking. As a result, the generalizations from this philosophical tradition often refer to universal and basic thinking activities, such as making comparisons and evaluations. The major defect of philosophical theorizing, says Sternberg, lies in overestimating the role of formal logic in critical thinking. Formal logic can only explain how people think under ideal circumstances and does not consider the concrete context in which thinking takes place. Therefore, it is a theory of competence in an ideal situation, a theory in which logical rules and categories dominate the landscape.

A *psychological theory* of critical thinking, on the other hand, is interested in "characterizing critical thinking as it is performed under the limitations of the person and the environment." (Sternberg, 1985) Many of the studies in the psychological tradition have been conducted by testing "one performance of human subjects in laboratory settings." (Sternberg, 1985) In comparison with the philosophical approach, the psychologists take into consideration the conditions that influence thinking. They are more interested in how well one thinks under specific circumstances, for example, when a teacher must decide how to discipline an errant child. As a consequence, they do not provide a rational model for thinking. Nonetheless, they can explain the variations observed in a model proposed by the philosophers. They can explain why the teacher who is challenged by an obnoxious student disciplines him out of her emotional state rather than making a decision from a list of logical alternatives.

A *pedagogical approach* to critical thinking is represented by figures like Bloom (1956), Perkins (1981), and Renzulli (1976) who are more directly bound up with the relation between critical thinking and school performance. They are more concerned with the "skills needed by children in the classroom for problem solving, decision making, and concept learning." (Sternberg, 1985) For example, can they identify critical questions? Can they list alternative solutions? Do they have standards to apply to the critical situation? Are they able to compare and contrast alternatives? Can they explain rationally the decision they have made?

Although the scholars from these three approaches contribute to theorizing about the nature of critical thinking, none of them has presented a thorough but practical model to guide teachers. All three traditions have brought with them some shortcomings characteristic of their respective disciplines.

In the philosophical tradition, the emphasis on formal logic leads philosophers to believe that "the rules of logic can tell us how people might think critically under ideal circumstances in which the limitations typically placed on the human information-processing system are not in place." (Sternberg, 1985) The psychological tradition, focusing on a specific performance, is limited by its laboratory and experimental base—on its case-study methodology. Although the educational tradition focuses on learning behavior and classroom teaching, it lacks the "clarity of epistemological status characteristic of the philosophical and psychological theories." (Sternberg 1985) Thus these three perspectives demonstrate that the study of critical thinking should not be limited to one or two disciplines.

Philosophy Directs Definition

Of the three traditions, the philosophical tradition has probably been the most influential, not only because the concept of critical thinking was originated by philosophers, but also because philosophical clarification is often considered essential to our understanding and interpretation of the world.

Robert Ennis was the first educational philosopher who attempted to define critical thinking for classroom teachers. Since the publication of his paper "The Concept of Critical Thinking" (1962), Ennis is viewed as the major proponent of the logical approach to critical thinking. He defines critical thinking as the "correct assessment of statements." It consists of a set of reasoning skills listed as the "twelve aspects of critical thinking."

1. Grasping the meaning of a statement.
2. Judging whether there is ambiguity in a statement.
3. Judging whether certain statements contradict each other.
4. Judging whether a conclusion follows necessarily.
5. Judging whether a statement is specific enough.
6. Judging whether a statement is actually the application of a certain principle.
7. Judging whether an observation is reliable.
8. Judging whether an inductive conclusion is warranted.
9. Judging whether the problem has been identified.
10. Judging whether something is an assumption.
11. Judging whether a definition is adequate.
12. Judging whether a statement made by an alleged authority is acceptable. (Ennis, 1962)

In addition to these twelve aspects, Ennis listed three dimensions of critical thinking: the logical dimension; the criterial dimension; and the pragmatic dimension.

As pointed out by others (McPeck, 1981; Siegel & Carey, 1989), Ennis' emphasis on logic is reflected in his definition of critical thinking. He emphasizes logic rather than beliefs. But Ennis does not think logic applied abstractly is sufficient. He claimed that specific content knowledge is necessary in order for a person to think critically. As we can see from the twelve aspects, without specific knowledge, most of them cannot be carried out.

McPeck challenges Ennis' definition of critical thinking because he believes it cannot fully demonstrate the true nature of critical thinking. Ennis' approach seems to ignore the fact that in actuality people vary their logic from one situation to another, and different fields of knowledge may require different types of thinking. McPeck maintains that critical thinking is subject specific, that is, the nature of the discipline and detailed knowledge of science makes its critical thinking different from critical thinking in social studies. There is, then, a subject-specific logic that must be used to think critically about that subject.

Discussing the meaning of critical thinking, McPeck generated ten features which can be summarized as follows:

1. Critical thinking is always subject dependent.
2. Critical thinking varies from field to field.
3. Critical thinking does not necessarily entail disagreement or rejection of accepted norms.
4. Critical thinking consists of the disposition and skill to reflect and seek truth in a given domain of knowledge.
5. Critical thinking is more than assessment of statement, it is a complex thought process involving problem solving and active engagement in certain activities.
6. The study of logic is not sufficient for critical thinking.
7. Since critical thinking is knowledge dependent, it is also knowledge limited.
8. The phrase "critical thinking" is both a 'task' and an 'achievement' phrase: does not necessarily imply success.
9. Critical thinking (in addition to the assessment of a statement) may also include the use or rejection of methods, strategies and techniques as examples.
10. Critical thinking is not coextensive with "rationality" but is a dimension of it. (McPeck, 1981)

McPeck's ten features attempt to bring together the logical or philosophical aspects of critical thinking with the cognitive or psychological aspects. He wants to broaden the definition of critical thinking to make it more than an analytic process. He doesn't say that critical thinking cannot be exercised when a person has limited knowledge about a subject, but he implies that limited knowledge limits or prohibits critical thinking.

To take an example from language arts/composition, a person who knows little about form and expository types will not be able to make critical judgments about the appropriateness of the form used in a particular essay. A person who has little or no knowledge about children's literature will have little to offer when comparing a new book to the array of children's books that have withstood the test of time. The closest McPeck comes to linking his ten features to classroom teaching is his notion that critical thinking is both a task and an achievement concept. If an achievement concept, it would seem that it could be described in performance terms, assessed, and reported. But McPeck's ten features do not include suggestions on how to assess critical thinking—a necessary coordinate of an instructional plan.

Since a knowledge base is a necessary ingredient in McPeck's concept of critical thinking, that puts him at odds with Paul's notion that methodology and strategy may be the focal point in teaching critical thinking.

Dialogical/Dialectical Mental Activities and Critical Thinking

At the heart of Richard Paul's method for critical thinking is what he calls *dialogical thinking*. Unlike most traditional philosophers, Paul sees dialogical thinking as an important dimension, as well as a characteristic, of critical thinking. By *dialogical*, Paul means that more than one frame of reference is contending for attention and settlement. It is the opposite of *monological*. In other words, dialogical thinking requires people to think with more than one alternative. These alternatives, or different frames of reference, will dialog with one another as the thinking process proceeds. If a reader thinks critically about a character in a story, he needs another character to compare; then a dialog can occur over the merits of character number one.

Closely related with dialogical thinking is *dialectical thinking*. Sometimes, the two terms are placed together like "dialogical/dialectical" thinking. The term "dialectical" "includes the ability to reflect critically on one's own thinking and the closely related ability to reason sympathetically within frames of reference distinct from, and even opposed to, one's own." (Rudinow & Paul, 1987) Simply put, *critical thinking for Paul is to be reflectively critical with oneself and sympa-*

thetically reasonable with others.

Paul makes a distinction between primary or instinctual and secondary or cultivated thinking. Primary thinking "is spontaneous, egocentric and strongly prone to irrational belief formation." (Paul, 1987) Therefore, the primary nature is instinctual and natural thinking that relies on feelings and beliefs. People acquire this type without any directed efforts or training.

Secondary thinking is characteristic of human goals and culture as a whole. It is acquired only through extensive training and systematic practice. In other words, it is acquired only through education and cultivation. The most obvious manifestation of this secondary thinking is human rationality, that is, an attempt to rise above instincts and feelings (beliefs). It is the goal of education to further the development of secondary thinking, of human rationality.

Dialogical thinking corresponds nicely to the anticipated dynamics in cooperative learning groups. Assuming the group has consolidated into a community of learners, a dialog about alternatives should arise each time a new decision has to be made by the group. Based on McPeck's features, however, the student with the most knowledge has the best opportunity to make critical judgments, assuming that person has the productive attitude that Norris claims makes critical thinkers in our classrooms.

Recent Books of Interest

Three books recently co-published by ERIC/RCS and NCTE on critical thinking discuss critical thinking as a process but not as a process related to the achievement or the application of specific strategies or skills. A basic assumption underlying those books equates critical thinking and rationality. Reading and understanding any text, therefore, requires some critical thinking, according to this position, because all extended text contains complexities for the mind that require it to use some of those mental manipulations that we usually call critical thinking skills.

In *Critical Thinking: A Semiotic Perspective*, Siegel and Carey (1989) base their theory about critical thinking on the seminal work of Charles Pierce. It is his notion that all thinking is in reality an interpretation of numerous signs that the thinker sees in the world around him. To drive thought beyond mere acceptance of the external meaning of signs, say Siegel and Carey, the thinker must adopt a cynical skepticism, a constant sense of disbelief. Critical thinking lies in the process of being skeptical, not in one or more specific behaviors that might be carved out.

The second book, *Critical Thinking and Reading: Empowering Learners to Think and Act* (Neilsen, 1989), extends the Pierce philosophy into John Dewey, who was influenced by Pierce. Dewey applied the notion of exploration and interpretation to an experimental school at the University of Chicago. It was there that he initiated what became known as the Progressive movement in education—progressive referring to its emphasis on individualism and the constant expansion of the individual towards achieving his own interests or goals.

The third book in the series, *Critical Thinking and Writing: Reclaiming the Essay* (Newkirk 1989), is a personal essay about the expository form called the personal essay. In it the author argues for a free-form for the personal essay, an openness of construction that will allow the mind to wander where it wants to go rather than trying to follow an artificial pattern taken from a book or from someone else's mind. This concept aligns Newkirk with the psychological definitions of critical thinking, meaning it is quite idiosyncratic. Newkirk believes that the personal essay should not be bound by external rules of logic but should explore the twists and turns that the individual mind takes. That allows the writer to follow his own lead, so to speak, but also allows the thinker to raise questions and to answer them as they occur, unencumbered by irrelevant textbook structures.

These three books have tried to blend philosophical and psychological aspects of critical thinking theory, but they provide no practical model for teachers. Teachers could certainly move from these ideas into classroom applications since all three books are predominantly psychological. They hold that the thinker maintains a skeptical attitude no matter what the content. They are philosophical in the sense that they are not grounded in laboratory studies and so operate from a priori assumptions. They are not rule-bound but certainly context-related—with special emphasis on the attitude and the status of the thinker.

Chapter 7

the reality of critical thinking

We wouldn't want to bring this discussion to a close without asking why we are concerned with critical thinking and critical reading. We educators sometimes get so involved in squabbles over methodology that we forget the purpose of our efforts—to provide our students with the knowledge and the intellectual skills to lead happy and productive lives. Clearly, that purpose involves making choices, and choices begin to differentiate our lives.

In order to make choices, students need more than a methodology. They need experience with significant ideas and with contrasting alternatives that affect lives, whether their own or others with whom they can identify. That's where literature, history, science and engineering enter the picture. They provide the knowledge, the events, the challenges of life that make it possible for students to evaluate life and to fit themselves into the picture.

There used to be a television program called "You Were There."

It was a series of reenactments of major historical events and the decisions that people of that moment had to make. Those dramas gave viewers the opportunity to think along with principal characters and to see what alternatives they had at critical decision points. The viewers vicariously became a part of a real life instance of critical thinking.

Those dramatized instances from history, from novels, from discoveries in science or from daily human relationships represent school sponsored opportunities for critical thinking. By reading about them and discussing alternative solutions, the teacher gives students safe experiences to practice critical thinking. They can then analyze methods or techniques for solving problems, i.e., thinking critically about the situation. They have to decide what to do or what to believe. That's when students and teachers can understand that history and literature are part of the ongoing stream of life, and they are in it. Being a critical thinker, a good decision maker, helps them swim more confidently in that stream. The job of the teacher is to provide students with a knowledge base and then help them examine it critically.

To the philosopher, logical systems seem to be the key to defining and understanding critical thinking. To the psychologist the context in which thinking takes place and the resulting attitude of the thinker are the important aspects. To the teacher the methodology for achieving critical thinking—however it may be observed—usually occupies center stage.

The oft-conflicting points of view described in this book give the classroom teachers leeway in defining and in teaching critical thinking. They could emphasize and teach the categories of skills that appear in the logical systems of Ennis or Paul. They could encourage the development of an attitude of disbelief for engaging in reflective thinking. They could identify particular behaviors, such as evaluating story form or applying values to a real-life situation, and teach those as specific examples of critical thinking.

Teachers also have the option of acting as model thinkers and then encouraging their students to imitate them, much as apprentices did in the craft guilds. Teachers can ask questions in a manner that stimulates students to challenge their own views and to compare their views with those of their peers. Teachers can follow a logical taxonomy of skills to give their students practice in comparing and contrasting, in establishing criteria, in judging worthiness, and in applying values to their own lives. These and other options are available to the teacher who wants to promote critical thinking and critical reading. The teacher's personality and philosophy will direct the choice.

It is our sense that most teachers are committed to serving the community in which they work. That means that they want to provide students and parents with performance evidence that their students are learning to think and to read critically. At the same time most teachers try to foster individual thought in each student. That means that they encourage students to adopt a broad attitude of inquiry and skepticism. This attitude, however, does not lend itself to easy assessment.

Even though the teaching of specific critical reading performance and the fostering of a broad attitude compete for the teacher's attention, they are not mutually exclusive. They do create, however, the kind of tension that makes the life of a teacher exciting. Those two goals prod the teacher to original thinking in answering the question: "How can I show critical thinking to the public while freeing my students to become academic detectives as they solve various problems?"

(Doesn't it seem appropriate for a book on critical thinking to end with a question?)

critical
thinking
activities

Recognizing Attitudes: Author's Viewpoint, Objective/ Subjective, Denotative/Connotative

(AUTHOR'S VIEWPOINT, OBJECTIVE/SUBJECTIVE)

OBJECTIVE
To develop students' ability to recognize the emotional attitude of a writer or speaker. To distinguish between objective and subjective statements.

PROCEDURE
Write on the board or prepare a handout with the following three statements:

1. "I'm enthusiastic over the prospect of a magnificent high rise and can see it soaring thirty-two stories into the sky on beams of reinforced concrete."

2. "I certainly support the building of a low-rent high rise and know that the property on Elm and Wood, which is now covered with dilapidated houses, would make an ideal location."

3. "If there were a high rise here at the edge of the business district, I'd like an apartment on the top floor so I could see the whole city."

Ask the students:

• Which of these statements was made by a real-estate agent?
• Which was made by a possible tenant?
• Which was made by a building contractor?

Point out that the real-estate agent, the tenant, and the contractor each looked at the project from his or her own viewpoint. Discuss why people view things from different perspectives.

Write *subjective attitude* on the board. Ask the students to define *subjective*. (Related to a particular person; personal; conditioned by how the person perceives reality.) After subjective attitude write *personal*. Ask the students to write on the handout or say out loud a subjective sentence about the high rise. Direct them to create a statement made by each of these persons:

- an unemployed construction worker
- a person who lives in a house marked for demolition by urban renewal
- a concrete manufacturer
- a person who has previously lived in a high rise.

Write *objective attitude* on the board. Ask the students to define *objective*. (Expressing the nature of reality apart from personal feeling.) After objective attitude write *impersonal*.

Ask the students to write or say an objective statement about a high rise. Note that these statements should not reveal how the writer or speaker feels about the high rise. Possible answers might be: A high-rise apartment building has elevators and many stories. The city council is discussing possible locations for a high-rise apartment.

Statements
Subjective
1. "Building a high rise would really help the economy. Lots of people like me could get work."

2. "All this city cares about is making money. They don't think about the people this high rise is going to displace."

Objective
1. "A high rise project will create one hundred new jobs."

2. "At twenty stories, it will be the third highest building in the city."

Sample statements on handout.

OBJECTIVE/SUBJECTIVE

OBJECTIVE

To distinguish between objective and subjective statements. To note both positive and negative subjective attitudes.

PROCEDURE

Write on the board or prepare a handout with the following sets of three sentences:

A. "The miserly old woman hoarded a fortune."

B. "The woman saved $200,000."

C. "Through good business sense the woman amassed tremendous wealth."

❧ ❧ ❧

D. "Jack has spent years collecting more than twenty toy robots from the 1930s and 1940s."

E. "Jack wisely invested his time in a collection of toy robots that is unusual and fascinating."

F. "Jack, a grown man, spends endless hours on a childish bunch of junky, old robots."

Ask the students which of the sentences in each group is the objective sentence. (Sentences B and D.) Point out that reporters usually write this type of factual, objective sentence. Ask the students why the other two sentences are subjective. Discuss the emotions and biases evident in each of the subjective sentences. How would the students describe the feelings of the writers? (Scornful, jealous, admiring, etc.)

Ask the students how they recognized the subjective attitudes of sentences A, C, E, and F. Have them point out which words suggest an emotional attitude, that is, which suggest positive or negative feelings.

State or have one student compose an objective sentence about your school or town. Ask other students to create subjective sentences, both positive and negative, to correspond with the objective statement. Have the students note words which reveal a positive or negative attitude. For example:

Objective: "Our class studies American history one period per day."

Subjective: "We spend a **long, boring** period **every single day** talking about **useless** things that happened a long time ago."

Subjective: "Each day our class spends an **enlightening** period **delving** into America's **exciting** past."

TEACHER'S NOTES

DENOTATIVE / CONNOTATIVE

OBJECTIVE
To develop students' ability to distinguish connotative and denotative meanings of words and recognize the use of connotative meanings in subjective sentences.

PROCEDURE
Write on the board *denotative meaning* and *connotative meaning*. Ask which of the following sentences probably gives the dictionary definition of *teenager*. (Sentence 3.)

1. A teenager is a hood.

2. A teenager is a young adult.

3. A teenager is a person between the ages of thirteen and nineteen.

Explain that this definition, which is not subjective, is called the denotative meaning. Every word has a denotative meaning given in the dictionary. However, words also carry connotative meanings given them by each person who uses them. Sentences 1 and 2 are examples of connotative meanings of the word *teenager*. Ask students how the writer of sentence 1 feels about teenagers. Do the same for sentence 2. Ask the students why the word *teenager* might connote different things to different people.

Discuss some of the following words which might have differing connotative meanings among the students: baby, war, female, patriotism, father, politics, socialist, welfare, taxes, boxing. Remind the students that they can always find the denotative meaning of a word in the dictionary.

Write the denotative meaning of a word on the board. Ask students to write or say out loud a connotative definition for the word which reveals a positive or negative attitude toward the word. For example:

- A snake is scaly, legless reptile.
- A snake _____ .

- A pacifist is a person strongly opposed to violence, especially war.
- A pacifist _____ .

- A home is a family's or a person's place of residence.
- A home _____ .

Discuss students' various answers.

TEACHER'S NOTES

Distinguishing Fact, Falsehood, and Fantasy

FACT, FALSEHOOD, FANTASY

OBJECTIVE
To distinguish fact from fantasy and falsehood from fantasy in statements and readings.

PROCEDURE
On the board write the following sentences:

1. My shoe pinched my toes and yelled, "Next time get a larger pair!"

2. These shoes are too small for my feet.

3. Shoes were first invented in 1950.

Ask the students which of the sentences is a statement of fact. (Sentence 2.) Ask what a fact is. (A deed which has been done; an event which has occurred; something that has actually happened or that has actual existence; something that can be verified; something that is known to have happened.) Ask what sentence 3 is. (It is a false statement or falsehood.) Point out that often statements sound factual but are not. Ask what a falsehood is. (An erroneous statement; a deceptive statement; an incorrect statement.) How can one prove whether a factual-sounding statement is true or false? (By examining the evidence.)

Ask what Sentence 1 is an example of. (A fanciful statement, or a fantasy.) Ask what a fantasy is. (A made-up, or make-believe, statement; a creation of the imagination; something that couldn't possibly have happened in the real world at the present time.) If students associate fantasy with falsehood, conduct a discussion of the difference between a factual-sounding but false statement and fantasy. Point out that a fantasy world in which animals talk or elves exist or unscientific things happen should not be equated with falsehood.

Ask the students why an author uses fantasy for telling a story. (Sometimes to entertain; sometimes because this technique would be more acceptable for the kind of truth the author is trying to convey.) Recall the story of *The Ugly Duckling.* Ask the students why Hans Christian Anderson chose to use fantasy to tell this story about becoming beautiful. (Because fantasy made the story more acceptable as well as more universal.)

Hand out to students or write on the board the following sets of sentences and have them identify which in each set is fact, which is factual-sounding but false, and which is fantastical.

Set A
1. Leaves make a rustling noise when the wind blows through them.

2. The leaves of trees have no practical function.

3. The leaves were whispering in the wind, "Winter's coming, winter's coming!"

Set B
1. Dinosaurs were found still living in the deep jungles of the Amazon rainforest in 1965.

2. Dinosaurs were so big that their footsteps caused earthquakes in prehistoric times.

3. Long ago, dinosaurs roamed the earth.

Have students compose their own sets of sentences addressing a single topic, writing one factual, one fantasy, and one false statement.

FACT AND FANTASY IN WRITING

OBJECTIVE

To distinguish between fact and fantasy in writing and understand purposes for use of fantasy as a writing technique.

PROCEDURE

If available in your newspaper, collect several columns by Art Buchwald or by Dave Barry. Have the students examine them for fact and fantasy. Discuss why the writers use fantasy in their writing. Does it make the writing more entertaining? Does it make it harder to understand the message? Are fantasy, satire, and humor good methods for delivering a serious or critical message?

THE FANTASY NOVEL

OBJECTIVE

To read a fantasy novel critically, noting factual and fantasy elements and analyzing the author's purpose.

PROCEDURE

Have the students read a book that is a fantasy. Possible choices are: *The Hobbit; Animal Farm; Gulliver's Travels; The Wizard of Oz; Slaughterhouse Five; Dr. Jekyll and Mr. Hyde; The Lion, the Witch, and the Wardrobe; Brave New World; Watership Down;* or others appropriate to your students' level.

Before reading, discuss the fact that the book is a fantasy. While they are reading, have the students think about how fantasy is used by the author and what kind of meaning may underlie the unreal settings, situations, and characters. Create a list of questions specific to the novel chosen for the students to think about as they read. Also have them note how factual or realistic settings, situations, and characters are sometimes mixed in with the fantastical ones. What real-world people, situations, or relationships are mirrored or explored in the fantasy novel? (These books of course can be used in numerous ways to develop critical thinking abilities.)

Distinguishing Fact from Opinion

(**FACT AND OPINION**)

OBJECTIVE

To distinguish statements of fact from statements of opinion.

PROCEDURE

Write the following statements on the board.

1. My dog weighs forty pounds.
2. Your dog weighs sixty-five pounds.
3. My dog knows how to fetch.

Tell the students that these sentences state facts. Ask them to define *fact*. (Something that has actually occurred or has actual existence; something that is known to have happened something that can be verified.) How can these facts be verified? (Weigh the dogs on a scale, demonstrate that the dog can fetch.)

Write the following sentences below the ones on the board.

1. My dog is a good dog.
2. My dog is better than your dog.
3. My dog is very intelligent.

Ask if these sentences are statements of fact. (No.) What are they? (Opinions.) What is an *opinion*? (A value judgment; an individual evaluation; a belief; an inference made from facts; a view; an appraisal.) Can these opinions be verified? (No.) Why not? (These are judgmental statements on which not all people would agree because of word connotations.)

Note that there is no general agreement on the exact meaning of qualitative words like good, bad, ugly, happy, pretty, beautiful, nice, honest, best, tall, short, small, big, etc. Ask the students questions like: What is a good dog? What does it mean to be intelligent? What do you mean by pretty? What makes a movie good? What is a great car? The students should have different opinions on the answers to these questions.

Write the following sentences on the board.

1. Maria is tall.
2. Maria is six feet two inches tall.
3. Thomas is nice.
4. Thomas helped his grandmother clean the kitchen.

Which sentences are facts? (Sentences 2 and 4.) How might the opinions expressed in sentences 1 and 3 have been inferred? (From the facts in sentences 2 and 4.)

Ask the students for statements of opinion and write them on the board. Ask them to change these opinion sentences to statements of fact. For example: "That novel is wonderful" could be stated "That novel won the critics' award." "My fish is small" could be stated "My fish is one inch long."

Write these three sentences on the board.

1. I think that France is the best country in the world.
2. France is my favorite country.
3. France is the best country in the world.

Ask the students if they see any differences between these sentences. (Sentence 3 is definitely an opinion. However, while the writer is stating an opinion in sentence 1, it is a fact that this is the writer's opinion. The writer is stating an opinion in sentence 2 also, but it is a fact that France is his or her favorite country.) There are fine distinctions here, so discuss this carefully.

(FACT AND OPINION IN EDITORIAL WRITING)

OBJECTIVE

To distinguish fact from opinion in an editorial and examine how facts are used to support opinion.

PROCEDURE

Split the class into groups and give each group copies of a different newspaper or magazine opinion or commentary article. Have each group read their article and identify sentences that express an opinion and sentences that state facts, sentences which support or relate to the opinion. Have each group report to the class on their article by summarizing the opinion of the writer and what facts the writer used to support his or her opinion.

To extend this activity have the group or the class discuss whether or not they agree with the opinion stated in the article(s). Ask students if they feel the writer gave sufficient facts to back up his or her opinion. Could the same facts be used to support a different or opposing viewpoint? Does it appear that the writer is interpreting facts according to a certain view of the world, or in terms of a certain belief system? Does it appear that the writer is stating only those facts that support his or her view and leaving out others that would not support it? If students do not agree with the article, have them back up their opposing point of view with supporting facts within their own knowledge, or by showing that the facts used by the writer can be interpreted in a different way.

Purposes for Reading

(**PURPOSES FOR READING/LIBRARY SKILLS**)

OBJECTIVE
To offer practice in using the library. To encourage students to think about the various purposes, including their own purposes, for reading.

PROCEDURE
Before a visit to the school library give each child a piece of paper containing two numbered items. Item one will be a written question, such as "What is the song of a whale?" Each child should receive a different question. Other questions could include:

"When and where did Mark Twain live?"
"What country in the world has the most people?"
"What is a Morgan horse?"
"How can I learn to fix my bicycle?"
"What is the name of a book about ballet dancers?"
"Who are some famous race car drivers?"
"What are the names of some animals that became extinct in this century?"
"Where do you go to learn to be an astronaut?"
"Where can I find a copy of the poem 'Stopping by Woods on a Snowy Evening' by Robert Frost?"
"Where can I find a copy of the poem 'Casey at the Bat' by Ernest Lawrence Thayer?"
"How does it feel to sail in a large ship across the ocean?"
"What was it like being an American soldier in World War I?"
"What was it like to be a slave before the Civil War?"
"How can people save gas when they drive?"

Leave space, at least two lines, after item one. Item two should be a blank line. Instruct the students to think of a question that they would like to find the answer to, information that they would like to find, or something they would like to know how to do. Ask them to write this as item number two on their papers. Tell the students that their assignment at the library will be to answer each question and to write how and/or where (in what book) they found the answer. Tell them to try to find answers on their own, but to ask for assistance from the library staff or you if they need help. If students can't answer their own questions, tell them to write down where they looked. Let them know that they can probably find the answer at a larger library.

The types and number of questions can vary depending on the grade level of your class and the amount of time available in the library. Formulate questions that can be answered with the resources in your library. Also try to avoid using only answers which can be found in the encyclopedia.

When they have returned to the classroom, ask a few students to share with the class one of their questions and how they found the answer. Have the students hand in their papers.

NAME_____

1. What is the song of a whale?

2._____

PURPOSES FOR WRITING AND READING

OBJECTIVE

To develop students' awareness of different purposes for writing and purposes for reading.

PROCEDURE

Locate two readings on a topic, one a factual article or encyclopedia-type entry, one a descriptive essay that includes personal and/or sensory images. Make a list of questions on the topic. Questions should include those that require objective factual answers, and those that require more subjective information. Have the class read the factual reading first. How many of the questions can be answered with this article. Read the second descriptive reading. Answer the remaining questions.

Possible readings could discuss places such as the Himalayas, the Sahara desert, the city of London, Buenos Aires, or New Delhi, or an archeaological dig; describe things like a comet, the sea, a tree; or describe experiences like the French revolution, life on a southern plantation, being a woman in Iran, etc.

Discuss with the class how the two readings differ. Ask them what the authors' purposes were for each. Have them note that there was more than one type of question on your list. Discuss why certain types of questions were answered with one reading and other types with the other. Have them note that the type of information they want or the type of questions they need to answer on a subject (that is, their purposes for reading) can determine the type of readings they need to consult.

(PERSONAL READING CHOICES)

OBJECTIVE

To encourage reading outside of assigned work. To encourage students to think about their purposes for reading and to consider whether or not those purposes are met.

PROCEDURE

Depending on the grade level and aptitude of your students, ask them to read one or more books of their own choosing per month. For each book read have the students fill out an index card with the name of the book, the author, and the type of book (e.g., autobiography, biography, science fiction, romance, historical fiction, how-to, science, etc.). Before reading the book the students should write on the card why they chose to read the book (e.g., for specific information, entertainment, favorite author, etc.). After reading the book students should then write whether or not they satisfied their purpose for reading the book. Did they find the information they wanted? Was this book as good as others by the same author? Did they find out how a famous person viewed their own life? Was the book what they expected? If not, was it worth reading anyway?, etc. Lastly, have students note whether or not they would recommend this to a friend and why. At the end of each month collect the cards to monitor the choices and remarks of the students. Encourage students to read numerous types of books, not all romances or all nonfiction, for example. Encourage them to keep the cards as a log of what they have read and to continue to build their log even after they have left your class.

Title: *And Then There Were None*   **Type of bk:** Murder
                                                            Mystery
Author: Agatha Christie
Reader's purpose: Like books by this author, enjoyment of good mystery.
After reading comments: Enjoyed book very much, lots of suspense, best Christie book I've read so far.
Recommend to a friend? Why?: Yes, very entertaining. Good mystery.

Title: *Improve Your Grades*   **Type of book:** nonfiction,
Author: Veltisezar B. Bautista   how-to
Reader's purpose: To learn how to study more effectively, to do better in school.
After reading comments: Book was fun to read, lots of good ideas. I think I will study more efficiently now.
Recommend to a friend? Why?: Definitely, it could help a lot of kids who aren't doing as well as they could in school.

To extend this activity, periodically have students write a full length book report on one of the books they have chosen. Here they can analyze and critique the book in more detail and at greater length. Have the focus of the report remain on their own purpose for reading the book and whether or not the book had value for them.

TEACHER'S NOTES

Controversy and Decision-Making

CONTROVERSY AND GROUP DECISION-MAKING

OBJECTIVE
To give students practice in understanding and weighing two sides of a controversial issue, discussing the issue in a group, and making a decision as a group.

PROCEDURE
Split the class into small groups. Hand out to each group articles representing two different sides of a controversial issue. Supply any factual information that might be necessary for a valid discussion. Choose issues which are within the students' ability to form an informed opinion.

For example:
- Should the United States and its allies have launched an attack on the Iraqi's in order to get them out of Kuwait?

- Should local property taxes be increased in order to provide more money to the school?

- Should universities divest in stock of companies that profit from tobacco products?

- Should lumber companies be stopped from logging old growth forests in the pacific northwest?

- Should smoking be banned from all public places?

- Should the death penalty be abolished?

- Should flag burning be illegal?

- Should your state, city, or town make recycling mandatory?
  etc.

Have each group study the two sides of the issue they have been assigned. Ask the students to make a list of arguments, first for one side, then for the other side of the controversy. They may use arguments from the articles they have been given and arguments offered by members of the group. When the lists are completed, instruct them to review the lists by seeing if each list contains counter arguments for every point made in the other list. Have them add any reasonable counter arguments to their lists. At this point, have the students summarize each position using the best arguments from their lists. When the students have formulated the best case they can for each side, have the group discuss the relative strength of the two sides. Instruct them to choose a side in the controversy based on the facts presented. Remind students to listen to all arguments regardless of their own position. When a decision has been made by the group, have them write a report that summarizes the issue, states their position with supporting evidence, and acknowledges but discounts arguments against their position.

The groups in the class can be assigned the same issue or different issues. Have the groups present their final reports to the class. If each group analyzes the same issue, see if all the groups come to the same conclusion. If they do, do they support it for the same reasons? If they don't, can one side persuade the other that they are wrong? If the groups analyze different issues, after hearing each group's report, does the class as a whole agree with their conclusions? Allow the class to ask questions of the members of the group.

> Throughout this activity encourage students to listen carefully to all opinions and facts. Remind them that they are discussing the worth of ideas, not of each other. If they already have an opinion on the issue or issues to be discussed, ask them to suspend their judgment until all arguments are presented.

SCIENCE AND SOCIETY

OBJECTIVE

To have students look at a controversial discovery or issue of the past or present in order to analyze the people and motives involved. To look at students' own personal beliefs and think about how they would act in such circumstances.

PROCEDURE

Three readings are suggested below. Have the class read any or all of them in order to engage in discussion of the controversies presented. Have them analyze the motives and actions of the people involved. How would they act if they were Galileo, Darwin, Scopes, etc.?

Suggested teacher introduction: Throughout history science has progressed as people have gradually built their knowledge of the world. Sometimes when discoveries are first made they are shocking or unacceptable to the people of the time in which they are made. Often the progress of scientific ideas has been slowed while discoveries where disputed, discounted, or hidden for political, religious, or other reasons.

1.   Galileo was a person persecuted for his ideas in his own time, but was later vindicated (he theorized that the sun, not the earth, is the center of the solar system, as Copernicus also hypothesized). Read a story or play about Galileo's life. Upper level students can read *The Recantation of Galileo Galilei* by Eric Bentley, or a translation of *Galileo* by Bertolt Brecht. Why did the church dispute Galileo's theories? Why did Galileo recant his scientific findings? Was Galileo wrong to recant? What do you think you would have done? Can students think of other examples of people who were ahead of their time? Did those people have similar experiences?

2.   Students may be aware that Charles Darwin's theory of evolution was rejected by some, because they felt it was in opposition to the

biblical version of creation. But today most people (though not all) believe that Darwin was basically right about evolution and natural selection. Have the students read an account of the Scopes trial, which took place in 1925. Jerome Lawrence and Robert E. Lee's play *Inherit the Wind* is one possibility. If desired, have students view the 1960 movie *Inherit the Wind*, which is based on the events surrounding the Scopes trial. Do they think that John Scopes should have been convicted? Are they surprised that Tennessee did not revoke its law prohibiting the teaching of evolution until 1967? Ask students if they think creationism should be required to be taught alongside evolution in American schools today. Why or why not? What about the beliefs of other religions? Could a person believe both in evolution and in what the Bible and some religions say about creation?

3. Have the class read an article or articles on the possible existence of extraterrestrial life or on the existence of UFO's. Some people believe in UFO's and extraterrestrial beings. Many even claim to have seen them. Perhaps they are mistaken, crazy, or they are lying. Perhaps they are telling the truth. Ask the students whether or not they believe that there is life in the universe other than on earth. Ask them to support their opinions. Are the students absolutely sure of their opinions, or do they think that future evidence may prove them right or wrong? If they were abducted by aliens, then returned to earth, what would they do?

Follow-up discussion: Ask the students if they always feel free to make up their own minds about certain issues. Do they sometimes feel compelled to go along with what others around them believe, even if they have different ideas? Other possible questions could include: If they made a scientific discovery that went against their country's, church's, or family's beliefs would they bring it out into the open and withstand the criticism and rejection of others? Can the students imagine a discovery that would be controversial today? If they had an experience with alien creatures or with the supernatural, what would they do? Do they think that people today can be as resistant to new ideas as the people of Galileo's time?

Thinking and Action

(TAKING ACTION ON SCARCE RESOURCES)

OBJECTIVE
To encourage students to think about a problem and to put their ideas into action.

PROCEDURE
Ask the students to think of resources that are costly, scarce or limited. Possible answers include water, land, oil, coal, natural gas, trees, electricity, paper, money.

Choose one or two of the resources mentioned. Explain why this is a resource that needs to be conserved. Ask: What are the benefits of using less? If the resource chosen is paper, some responses might be: "Save money.", "Save trees.", "Pollute less.", etc. Ask the students: How do we use paper? Have the students think of how it is used at school and at home. Responses may include: "To write on.", "To make books.", "To make bags and packages for things.", etc. Write a list of the answers on the board.

Next ask the students to think of ways they could cut down on use of this resource. For example: "Use both sides of a sheet of paper.", "Do math problems in pencil so that mistakes can be erased.", "Use sheets of paper that are just big enough for the purpose, not bigger.", "Cut up scrap paper to write phone messages or notes on at home.", "Reuse paper bags.", etc.

Lastly, put some of their suggestions into practice in the classroom. Post the list of resource uses and the list of ways to save on the bulletin board. Ask students to try to follow the suggestions at home too. Encourage the students to give you suggestions on ways to save resources throughout the year.

CAREERS: PREPARING FOR ACTION

OBJECTIVE

To encourage students to think about and plan for careers. To develop research skills and encourage students to go beyond typical library sources.

PROCEDURE

Ask students to think about what kind of job or career they would like to have when they are older. Perhaps they have a number of ideas, but are not sure. Let them choose one to pursue for this activity. By learning more about the job or career they may have a better idea about whether it is really right for them.

After each student has chosen a profession to investigate, tell them to take a trip to the library to find information. Have them look for books and articles about their career and about careers in general. If there are associations of people in their line of work, have the students write to the associations requesting information. Give the students a list of specific questions to guide their research. Questions can include:

1. What is the job or career you are interested in?
2. Why are you interested in it?
3. How will you train for this job?
4. What kinds of skills are necessary to do well in this job?
5. What do people do in this job?
6. What is a typical work day like in this job?
7. Does this job pay well?
8. Where can this job be done? Anywhere?
9. Does this career fit in with other goals you have in your life?
10. Can you see any problems you might encounter in trying to pursue this career?
11. What can you do while you are still in school to prepare for this job?

Have the students answer as many of these questions as they can and add any other pertinent information. Allow students plenty of time to work on this assignment. Give them time to write letters and receive responses. They may also wish to interview adults they know who work at the job they are interested in or visit the work site of someone in the job.

If the job requires special training, a college degree, or graduate school, have the students find out some good institutions to attend. They may get information on these schools, their entrance requirements, costs, number of years required, etc.

Ask them to write a report on the information they have found and write a plan of action for someone who wants to pursue this career. Have them include in their paper a discussion of why this career would (or would not) suit them. In this section they can talk about their positive or negative feelings toward this career. They can also assess their own skills, strengths and weaknesses in relation to the career.

Students will have informed themselves about the steps they need to take to make their career goals come true. Some students may find that after carefully researching the job, they are no longer interested in it. This is a valuable lesson too. Encourage students to think ahead about jobs they are interested in. This activity should help them to realize that if they don't plan ahead they may hurt their chances to do the things that interest them.

TEACHER'S NOTES

(PROBLEM SOLVING AND ACTION)

OBJECTIVE
To develop problem solving and critical thinking skills in students by having them think about a problem, articulate ideas about solutions, and carry through their solution(s) by taking action.

PROCEDURE
1. Choose a current problem or topic of concern for students to discuss. Select a problem about which the students themselves could take some action.
2. State the problem for the class, providing readings and information necessary for a good understanding amongst the students.
3. Hold a classroom brainstorming session where solutions and steps can be offered by the students. Record the various ideas on the board.
4. When all ideas have been stated, discuss their relative merits. Which are practical, which will make a difference? Are the ideas consistent with each other, or must a choice be made between a number of courses of action?
5. Have the students make a decision regarding the best action or actions to take.
6. Spell out a plan of action to be followed.
7. Have students monitor fulfillment and success of the class plan.

Possible topics and actions:

Topic	Actions
Environmental/conservation problems	recycle classroom materials; recycle at home; write to politicians to encourage protection of wildlife, or national energy conservation program; raise money for environmental group whose goals they support

Poor discipline in the school cafeteria	editorial in school newspaper; peer pressure to behave; decorate cafeteria
No money for a class trip	look into fund raising possibilities; choose one, set a goal; get support of families and friends; ask for support from local business
Drug use by young people	students educate themselves; create student support system, hotline, peer counseling; publish information in school paper; organize school activities

TEACHER'S NOTES

Responding to Literature

READING AND WRITING DESCRIPTIVE POETRY

OBJECTIVE

To widen students' perceptions by critically analyzing descriptive poetry and by writing their own.

PROCEDURE

Have the class read and discuss a few descriptive poems. Distinguish descriptive poems from narrative and other types of poetry. Have the students note the word choice of the author and the use of other literary devices. What kind of evocative language is used? What kinds of images are conjured up by the poem? What senses are engaged? Did the poem make them think or feel differently about its subject than they had before? Did it make them look at the subject in a new way? (Examples of descriptive poems include: "Cats!" by Eleanor Farjeon, "Fog" by Carl Sandburg, "City: San Francisco" by Langston Hughes, "The Eagle" by Alfred, Lord Tennyson.)

Ask the students to compose a descriptive poem. Have them think carefully about what they want their poem to be about. It should be something that brings up strong feelings or images for them. Have them try to engage the senses of the reader by using descriptive words that have strong evocative powers. Have the students share their poems with the class. Note the great range in subject matter. Ask the students to try to feel what each writer is trying to say, to put themselves in the place of the writer. Even though the subject of the poem is not the writer, does the poem tell them something about the writer?

(LETTERS TO LITERARY CHARACTERS)

OBJECTIVE

To encourage students to think about literary characters by communicating with them and analyzing them on a personal basis.

PROCEDURE

After reading a story or book have your students choose a main character and write a personal letter to that character. Ask them to tell the character about themselves and about any similarities they share. Have them write about what they admire in the character or why they sympathize with the character. If they dislike the character or the actions and decisions of the character, they can write about this too. Suggest that they include any questions that they would like to ask the character.

This activity can be used with students of any level. It may work especially well if the characters are approximately the same age as the students, though this is not an absolute.

If desired, this activity can be extended by asking the students to write responses by the book characters to their own letters. Ask them to place themselves in the position of the character. Have them answer any questions and respond to any sympathy or criticisms contained in the first letter.

Some possible books with which to use this activity:

Madeline by Ludwig Bemelmans
Sam, Bangs and Moonshine by Evaline Ness
Charlotte's Web by E. B. White
Johnny Tremain by Esther Forbes
The Black Stallion by Walter Farley
The Diary of Anne Frank by Frances Goodrich and Albert Hackett
My Side of the Mountain by Jean George
The Heart is a Lonely Hunter by Carson McCullers
To Kill a Mocking Bird by Harper Lee
Little Women by Louisa May Alcott
The Outsiders by S. E. Hinton
Summer of My German Soldier by Bette Greene
Lord of the Flies by William Golding

Using Entertainment Media for Critical Thinking

PROBLEM SOLVING IN TV PROGRAMS

OBJECTIVE

To encourage students to look at television programming more critically, to set personal standards, and to develop problem solving skills.

PROCEDURE

Ask students to view two TV shows over the course of a week. These shows can include sitcoms, dramas, action/adventure—anything with a storyline. Game shows and news reports are not appropriate for this activity. Give them a sheet of paper for each show with the following questions to answer:

1. Name of TV show
2. Type of show
3. Setting of show
4. Main characters in show/episode
5. What problem arises in this episode?
6. How is the problem resolved?
7. How would you have solved this problem if it were your problem?
8. Is the show realistic?
9. What makes it realistic or not realistic?
10. Is it important for this type of show to be realistic?

Add other questions that you think are appropriate. On the back of the sheet have the students write a brief personal assessment of the show. Do they like this show? Why, why not? What value does it have for them? (Entertaining, funny, exciting, educational?)

Before turning in their papers, have the class discuss a few of the shows viewed and the students' responses. Is there disagreement among class members over the problem resolution and assessment of the TV shows?

GET MACGYVER OUT OF TROUBLE

OBJECTIVE
To make use of students' interest in television to promote creative writing and problem solving skills.

PROCEDURE
Ask students if they are familiar with the *MacGyver* TV program. Fill in those who aren't. Perhaps show a taped episode of *MacGyver* in class to the students. MacGyver is a character who gets into all sorts of seemingly impossible situations wherein he must use his incredible ingenuity to save himself or do what needs to be done. In addition to being extremely resourceful, he is a very good guy, always honest and compassionate.

Write the beginning of a make-believe *MacGyver* episode. Set up the situation and problem. The students' writing assignment will be to write the second half of the episode. They must use their imaginations to figure out how MacGyver will cleverly get out of the jam that you have gotten him into. Don't insist on perfect realism (the program doesn't), but ask the students to be as realistic as possible. Have the writers of a few of the best or most original read their compositions in class.

TEACHER'S NOTES

LITERATURE AND FILMS

OBJECTIVE

To develop students' critical skills by comparing and contrasting literature in its original form and as adapted for the screen.

PROCEDURE

After reading Shakespeare's *Henry V, Hamlet,* or *Romeo and Juliet* have the class view the movie. (Both *Henry V* and *Hamlet* have been done quite recently.) Or have the class read *Dances With Wolves, White Fang, Gone With the Wind, Lord of the Flies, Ordinary People* or another novel that has been adapted for the screen.

Have the students compare the two versions. Ask questions such as: Was the movie true to the original novel or play? What were some differences? Did changes alter the mood or meaning of the story? Which version did you prefer? Why? Did the characters in the movie look and act like you had pictured the characters to look and act when you read the play or novel? Which version told you more about the characters and their motivations?

Ask students to think about and discuss the relative strengths and weaknesses of the two media—the written word and the film. Is one more limited than the other? Or are they simply limited in different ways?

If you maintain a classroom library for students' personal reading, be sure to include copies of books that have been recently made into films or TV movies. They are likely to be especially interesting to many students. Their availability will encourage even reluctant readers to read when it is not required.

references

Baldwin, R. S., et al. "Effects of Topic Interest and Prior Knowledge on Reading Comprehension." *Reading Research Quarterly* Vol. 20, No. 4 (Sum 1985) pp. 497-504.

Belloni, L. F. and Jongsma, E. A. "The Effects of Interest on Reading Comprehension of Low-Achieving Students." *Journal of Reading* Vol. 22, No. 2 (Nov 1978) pp. 106-109.

Bloom, B. S., ed. *Taxonomy of Educational Objectives Handbook I: Cognitive Domain.* New York: David McKay Company, 1956.

Boyer, E. L. *High School: A Report on Secondary Education in America.* New York: Harper & Row, 1983.

Ennis, R. H. "A Concept of Critical Thinking." *Harvard Educational Review* Vol. 32, No. 2 (1962) pp. 81-111.

Ericson, B., et al. "Increasing Critical Reading in Junior High Classrooms." *Journal of Reading* Vol. 30, No. 5 (Feb 1987) pp. 430-39.

Falkof, L. and Moss, J. "When Teachers Tackle Thinking Skills." *Educational Leadership* Vol. 42, No. 3 (Nov 1984) pp. 4-9.

Flesch, R. *Why Johnny Can't Read and What You Can Do About It.* New York: Harper & Row, 1955.

Harris, L. and Smith, C. *Reading Instruction*. New York: Macmillan, 1987. Some of the ideas presented in *A Commitment to Critical Thinking* were previously published in *Reading Instruction*.

Harste, J. "Preface." In Siegel and Carey *Critical Thinking: A Semiotic Perspective*. Monograph Series on Teaching Critical Thinking, No. 1. Bloomington, IN: ERIC/RCS; Urbana, IL: NCTE, 1989.

Johnson, R. T. and Johnson, D. W. "Action Research: Cooperative Learning in the Science Classroom." *Science and Children* Vol. 24, No. 2 (Oct 1986) pp. 31-32.

Lew, M., et al. "Components of Cooperative Learning: Effects of Collaborative Skills and Academic Group Contingencies on Achievement and Mainstreaming." *Contemporary Education Psychology* Vol. 11, No. 3 (1986) pp. 229-39.

Lipman, M. "Critical Thinking—What Can It Be?" *Educational Leadership* Vol. 46, No. 1 (Sep 1988) pp. 38-43.

McPeck, J. E. *Critical Thinking and Education*. Oxford: Martin Robertson & Company, 1981.

Meehan, T. "The Effects of Instruction Based on Elements of Critical Reading Upon the Questioning Patterns of Pre-service Teachers." Ed.D. Dissertation, Indiana University, Bloomington, 1970.

Neilsen, A. R. *Critical Thinking and Reading: Empowering Learners to Think and Act*. Monograph Series on Teaching Critical Thinking, No. 2. Bloomington, IN: ERIC/RCS; Urbana, IL: NCTE, 1989.

Newkirk, T. *Critical Thinking and Writing: Reclaiming the Essay*. Monograph Series on Teaching Critical Thinking, No. 3. Bloomington, IN: ERIC/RCS; Urbana, IL: NCTE, 1989.

Norris, S. P. "Synthesis of Research on Critical Thinking." *Educational Leadership* Vol. 21, No. 8 (1985) pp. 40-45.

Paul, R. W. "Dialogical Thinking: Critical Thought Essential to the Acquisition of Rational Knowledge and Passions." In Baron and Sternberg (Eds.) *Teaching Thinking Skills: Theory and Practice.* New York: Freeman, 1987.

Perkins, D. N. *Mind's Best Work.* Cambridge, MA: Harvard University Press, 1981.

Ratekin, N., et al. "Why Teachers Resist Content Reading Instruction." *Journal of Reading* Vol. 28, No. 5 (Feb 1985) pp. 432-37.

Renzulli, J. S., et al. *Scales for Rating the Behavioral Characteristics of Superior Students.* Wethersfield, CT: Creative Learning Press, 1976.

Robinson, H. M. "Developing Critical Readers." In R. G. Stauffer (Ed.) *Dimensions of Critical Reading.* Newark, NJ: University of Delaware, Proceedings of the Annual Education and Reading Conference, 1964.

Rosenblatt, L. M. *Literature as Exploration.* New York: Noble and Noble, 1976.

Rudinow, J. and Paul R. W. "A Strategy for Developing Dialectical Thinking Skills." In Heiman and Slomianko (Eds.) *Thinking Skills Instruction: Concepts and Techniques.* Building Students' Thinking Skills Series., Washington, D. C.: National Education Association, 1987.

Rumelhart, D. E. "Schemata: The Building Blocks of Cognition." In R. J. Spiro, B. C. Bruce, & W. F. Brewer (Eds.) *Theoretical Issues in Reading Comprehension.* Hillsdale, NJ: Lawrence Erlbaum, 1980.

Russell, D. H. *Children's Thinking.* Boston: Ginn and Company, 1956.

Siegel, M. and Carey, R. F. *Critical Thinking: A Semiotic Perspective* . Monograph Series on Teaching Critical Thinking, No. 1. Bloomington, IN: ERIC/RCS; Urbana, IL: NCTE, 1989.

Slavin, R. E. "Cooperative Learning and the Cooperative School." *Educational Leadership* Vol. 45, No. 3 (Nov 1987) pp. 7-13.

Sternberg, R. J. "Teaching Critical Thinking, Part 1: Are We Making Critical Mistakes?" *Phi Delta Kappan* Vol. 67, No. 3 (Nov 1985) pp. 194-98.

Stotsky, S. "Imagination, Writing, and the Integration of Knowledge." Revised version of a paper presented at the Annual Meeting of the New England Association of Teachers of English, Bedford, NH, Oct 1983.

Wheeler, R. and Ryan, F. L. "Effects of Cooperative and Competitive Classroom Environments on the Attitudes and Achievement of Elementary School Students Engaged in Social Studies Inquiry Activities." *Journal of Educational Psychology* Vol. 65, No. 3 (Dec 1973) pp. 402-407.

annotated
bibliography

This bibliography contains 56 annotated resources related to critical thinking from the ERIC database. Two types of citations are included in this bibliography—citations to ERIC documents and citations of journal articles. The distinction between the two is important only if you are interested in obtaining the full text of any of these items. To obtain the full text of ERIC documents, you will need the ED number given in square brackets following the citation. For approximately 98% of the ERIC documents, the full text can be found in the ERIC microfiche collection. This collection is available in over 800 libraries across the country. Alternatively, you may prefer to order your own copy of the document from the ERIC Document Reproduction Service (EDRS). You can contact EDRS by writing to 7420 Fullerton Road, Suite 110, Springfield, Virginia 22153–2852 or by telephoning them at (800) 443–3742.

Full text copies of journal articles are not available in the ERIC microfiche collection or through EDRS. Articles can be acquired most economically from library collections or through interlibrary loan. Articles from some journals are also available through University Microfilms International at (800) 732–0616 or through the Original Article Tearsheet service of the Institute for Scientific Information at (800) 523–1850.

Activities to Promote Critical Thinking. Classroom Practices in Teaching English. Prepared by the NCTE Committee on Classroom Practices in Teaching English, National Council of Teachers of English, Urbana, IL. 1986. 158 pp. [ED273985]

Intended to involve students in language and communication study in such a way that significant thinking occurs, this collection of teaching ideas outlines ways to teach literature and composition that engage the students in such thinking processes as inferring, sequencing, predicting, classifying, problem solving, and synthesizing. The activities are divided into categories for composition, speaking and listening, literature study, additional creative and critical thinking activities, and speaking and writing across the curriculum.

Allen, Elizabeth Godwin; and others. "Using Language Experience to ALERT Pupils' Critical Thinking Skills." *Reading Teacher*, v41 n9 May 1988, pp. 904-910 [EJ370158]

Describes the "ALERT" procedure, whereby teachers combine the language experience approach with the use of radio, television, newspaper, and magazine advertisements in a strategy that develops critical thinking skills, even in very young students.

Alvarez, Marino C. *Knowledge Activation and Schema Construction.* Paper presented at the Annual Meeting of the American Educational Research Association (Boston, MA, April 16-20, 1990). 28 pp. [ED317988]

This study examined how instruction that encourages critical thinking about what has been read can lead to incorporated knowledge that can be retrieved and applied to other related settings. Case-based learning (a method long used with graduate business, law, and medical students) is one method that can be used to foster critical thinking and schema construction. For this study, a case was defined as a narrative that presented a theme portrayed in a novel but presented it in a problem-solving format that related text ideas to real-world situations. The effects of case based instruction were compared to those of traditional instruction on students' ability to assemble and incorporate different knowledge sources in memory. Ninety-two ninth graders in a rural community participated in the 6-week study. Students read the novel "To Kill a Mockingbird" and were evaluated by their written responses to essays and timed writings. Findings indicated that the use of thematically organized and cross-disciplinary cases facilitated students' ability to generate explanations for new information that were plausible and meaningful.

Ashby-Davis, Claire. "Improving Students' Comprehension of Character Development in Plays." *Reading Horizons*, v26 n4 Sum 1986. pp. 256-61 [EJ337364]

Presents a method for improving reading comprehension through direct instruction of inductive reasoning. Students gather clues to personality of characters as play progresses and arrive at an overall generalization concerning the complexities of the character.

Baldwin, R. Scott; and others. "Effects of Topic Interest and Prior Knowledge on Reading Comprehension." *Reading Research Quarterly*, v20 n4 Sum 1985. pp. 497-504 [EJ319729]

Reports on a study that examined the effects of prior knowledge and topic interest on the reading comprehension of seventh- and eighth-graders. The results suggested that both prior knowledge and topic interest were autonomous factors in reading comprehension.

Borasi, Raffaella; Siegel, Marjorie. "Reading To Learn Mathematics: A New Synthesis of the Traditional Basics." Paper presented at the Annual Meeting of the American Educational Research Association (San Francisco, CA, March 27-31, 1989). 32 pp. [ED305612]

Reading to learn mathematics forges a new synthesis of the traditional basics of reading and mathematics which aims at fostering critical thinking and may provide an instructional context within which students and teachers can work out meaningful conceptions of mathematics. Benefits of this synthesis include: (1) contributing to better learning and understanding of mathematical content; (2)

developing new learning strategies useful in new learning situations; and (3) developing a deeper understanding of mathematics as a discipline. Reading to learn mathematics may be able to play a role in bringing about much needed reform of the mathematics curriculum and to a reconceptualization of the role of the traditional "basics" in educating students as critical thinkers.

Commeyras, Michelle. *Analyzing a Critical-Thinking Reading Lesson.* Technical Report No. 464. Bolt, Beranek and Newman, Cambridge, MA; Illinois Univ., Urbana. Center for the Study of Reading. 1989 [ED304680]

To illustrate the relationship between critical thinking and reading comprehension, and to show that critical thinking can be infused into classroom instruction using ordinary classroom materials, a study analyzed the transcript of a critical-thinking reading lesson for sixth grade students. Students read a story independently and completed a written assignment before meeting to discuss the story. The assignment entailed gathering evidence to support two different hypotheses about the story that would be considered in the discussion. Analysis revealed that students used critical thinking when given the opportunity. Students gave reasons that could serve as evidence for two explanatory hypotheses, supported their judgments when they evaluated the strength of those reasons, and made inferences which integrated background knowledge with textual information.

Commeyras, Michelle. "Using Literature to Teach Critical Thinking." *Journal of Reading,* v32 n8 May 1989. pp. 703-707 [EJ388545]

Provides a rationale for using fiction and drama to promote critical thinking. Presents a sample grid used to record answers to and interpretations of six questions which can be used in class discussion to bring out critical thinking dispositions, such as the ability to determine whether a generalization is warranted.

Contee, Carmen; Gerhard, Christian. "The Big Shift: From Traditional High School Reading Program to a Thinking Skills Program." Paper presented at the Annual Meeting of the International Reading Association (31st, Philadelphia, PA, April 13-17, 1986). 12 pp. [ED276989]

Initial activities in a collaborative reading project for tenth graders were based on the categorizing process, which is the basis for understanding the structure of ideas in most textbooks. Ideas are organized in a hierarchy of related categories moving down from the title, through chapter headings, main headings, subheadings, to paragraphs. Students practiced categorizing objects before they were introduced to the textbook, and they then applied their categorizing skills to reading the textbook—an eleventh grade history text. Some of the results were as follows: (1) attendance in reading classes and behavior in class improved dramatically; (2) the writing of well-organized, structured paragraphs also improved; (3) students were able to analyze different types of relationships; and (4) students gained confidence in their ability to know how to approach textbook material and read efficiently for different purposes.

Dedicott, Wendy. "The Value of Pictures in Encouraging Children's Thinking Strategies." *Reading*, v21 n1 Apr 1987. pp. 53-61 [EJ352219]

Describes a project in which different kinds of pictures were used to promote children's thinking and language skills.

Doyle, Michelle L. "This 'Buzz' Has Wings!" *Momentum*, v19 n4 Nov 1988. pp. 48-50 [EJ382589]

Describes the Critical Writing Program in the Catholic elementary schools in Arlington, Virginia, which teaches critical thinking through the process of writing. Illustrates the application of critical writing to history, science, and other subjects. Suggests ideas for "publishing" students' writing.

Duke, Leona R. "Teaching the Accepted Methods of Your Profession: The Teacher as Risk Taker." *English Journal*, v75 n5 Sep 1986. pp. 53-55 [EJ339910]

Criticizes school policies that hamper teachers' use of new methods such as journal writing and reader response to literature because these methods have caused criticism of teachers and school administrators. Concludes that students have a right to ideas, good teaching, sharing, mistakes, and trust.

Educators: Try NIE. American Newspaper Publishers Association Foundation, Washington, D.C. [ED309428]

This pamphlet promotes the Newspaper in Education (NIE) program. It discusses reasons why educators should choose newspapers as instructional tools; how they can be used for individualized instruction, reading, writing, computing, and critical thinking; what the research says about the use of newspapers in schools; what services are available through NIE; and how to get an NIE program started.

Ellis, Thomas I. "Teaching Thinking Skills." *Research Roundup,* v4 n3 Apr 1988. National Association of Elementary School Principals, Alexandria, VA. Prepared by the ERIC Clearinghouse on Educational Management, University of Oregon, Eugene. 6 pp. [ED295302]

This pamphlet reviews five reports that highlight an emerging consensus among researchers about the value of systematically incorporating cognitive instruction into the elementary school curriculum. First is a comprehensive framework for an integrated approach to thinking skills. Next are three research studies conducted at the elementary level that reveal the efficacy of cognitive instruction both in raising achievement levels and in closing the gap between high and low achievers. The final selection describes the development and implementation of a successful cognitive instruction program for kindergarten through third grade in an urban school district.

Ericson, Bonnie; and others. "Increasing Critical Reading in Junior High Classrooms." *Journal of Reading,* v30 n5 Feb 1987. pp. 430-39 [EJ346895]

Describes three content area reading strategies, anticipation-reaction guides, text previews, and three-level study guides, that capitalize on cooperative small group learning and emphasize higher order critical thinking.

Estaville, Lawrence E., Jr. "Debate: A Teaching Strategy for Geography." *Journal of Geography*, v87 n1 Jan-Feb 1988. pp. 2-4 [EJ369573]

States that classroom debate can stimulate students to think critically about important issues and strengthen their abilities to express ideas logically. Outlines a teaching strategy that uses a debate format to improve students' verbal and their writing skills.

Falkof, Lucille; Moss, Janet. "When Teachers Tackle Thinking Skills." *Educational Leadership*, v42 n3 Nov 1984. pp. 4-9 [EJ310024]

Describes a district-wide thinking skills program developed by teachers in an Illinois elementary school.

Farnan, Nancy. "Critical Reading and Writing through a Reader Response Approach." *Writing Teacher*, v2 n5 Apr-May 1989. pp. 36-38 [EJ396456]

Outlines the importance of a literature-based curriculum that encourages higher-order thinking skills. Discusses the reader-response approach to language arts teaching as a valuable instructional process, that emphasizes the connections between what is in a text and the reader's previous knowledge and experience, thus fostering higher-order thinking skills.

Fox, Carol; Sauer, Margery. *Celebrate Literature! A Spiraling Curriculum for Grades K-6.* Elgin School District 46, IL 1988. 15 pp. [ED297265]

"Celebrate Literature!," a multi-volume articulated literature curriculum for grades K-6, intended to foster students' awareness of their literary heritage, increase their knowledge of story structure and provide examples of excellence in children's literature, is described in this paper. By building upon established practices of reading aloud to children, the curriculum offers teachers information about genre, books, authors, and illustrators and provides a structure for using children's literature in the classroom.

Goldstone, Bette P. "Visual Interpretation of Children's Books." *Reading Teacher,* v42 n8 Special Issue: Empowering Both Teachers and Students. Apr 1989. pp. 592-95 [EJ386928]

Examines how visual literacy (the ability to interpret the visual images of advertisements, illustrations, television, and other visual media) can promote creative and analytic thinking. Provides several instructional strategies to teach visual literacy through book illustrations. Notes that visual literacy is essential in a world increasingly dominated by visual messages.

Haggard, Martha Rapp. "Developing Critical Thinking with the Directed Reading-Thinking Activity." *Reading Teacher,* v41 n6 Feb 1988. pp. 526-33 [EJ367179]

Recognizes that many teachers feel uncomfortable with the Directed Reading Thinking Activity (DRTA). Describes and explains the steps, or elements, of the DRTA and suggests ideas for preparing and implementing this instructional strategy.

Hickey, Gail. "Creative Activities for Fostering Critical Reading in Elementary Social Studies." *Georgia Social Science Journal,* v19 n2 Fall 1988. pp. 20-21 [EJ392917]

Suggests activities for fostering critical reading skills in social studies. Activities include assigning reporting roles to students; asking students to create a cartoon or slogan; having students to review a favorite television program; and helping students identify exaggeration.

Idol, Lorna. "A Critical Thinking Map to Improve Content Area Comprehension of Poor Readers." *Remedial and Special Education (RASE),* v8 n4 Jul-Aug 1987. pp. 28-40 [EJ359379]

A mapping strategy for thinking critically about expository text, focusing on the passage's main idea, major supporting points, other viewpoints, reader's conclusion, and relevance to a contemporary situation, was effective in improving reading comprehension of four high school sophomores in a remedial reading class and two mildly mentally retarded high school juniors.

Johnson, Roger T.; Johnson, David W. "Action Research: Cooperative Learning in the Science Classroom." *Science and Children,* v24 n2 Oct 1986. pp. 31-32 [EJ341892]

Promotes the Every Teacher a Researcher program of the National Science Teachers Association. Encourages teachers to become involved in three types of action research with regard to cooperative learning in science. These are replicating, refining, and extending. Includes program registration form for interested teachers.

Karolides, Nicholas J., Ed. "Beyond the Two R's." *Wisconsin English Journal,* v29 n2 Wisconsin Council of Teachers of English. Jan 1987. 36 pp. [ED280027]

The compendium of articles in this journal issue deal with the diverse components of the language arts, communication, and critical thinking curricula. Also included in this journal are a list of the NCTE Achievement Awards winners, as well as reviews of selected books for children, adolescents, and for teachers.

Kruse, Janice; Presseisen, Barbara Z. *A Catalog of Programs for Teaching Thinking.* Research for Better Schools, Philadelphia, PA 46 pp. [ED290125]

Designed to reach a varied audience, this catalog provides concise summaries of some of the major commercial programs that teach thinking, and furnishes descriptions in terms of major goal, target audience, assumptions, process/materials, time, and developer. The first section offers programs primarily intended for teachers, including the California Writing Project, cognitive levels matching, critical thinking, and tactics for thinking. The next section supplies summaries of available materials for students at various levels, including building thinking skills, future problem solving, Great Books, philosophy for children, and strategic reasoning. The final section furnishes material for specific age groups—elementary, middle school, and secondary students. Publisher and/or developer addresses are given for each program, as well as a cost estimate for the materials mentioned.

Kuhrt, Bonnie L.; Farris, Pamela J. "Empowering Students through Reading, Writing, and Reasoning." *Journal of Reading*, v33 n6 Mar 1990. pp. 436-41 [EJ405088]

Argues that teachers can determine the instructional frameworks which can empower students to understand more about their own learning. Describes activities (learning logs, directed reading-thinking activities) that develop higher level thinking skills using writing, reading, and reasoning. Concludes that such activities facilitate students' metacognitive awareness.

Lew, Marvin; and others. "Components of Cooperative Learning: Effects of Collaborative Skills and Academic Group Contingencies on Achievement and Mainstreaming." *Contemporary Educational Psychology*, v11 n3 Jul 1986. pp. 229-39 [EJ338404]

This study investigates the impact of cooperative learning and the impact of opportunity to interact with classmates on achievement and cross-handicap relationships. Results indicate that positive goal interdependence with collaborative-skills and academic group contingencies promoted positive relationships with nonhandicapped classmates, frequent engagement in cooperative skills, and highest achievement.

Lipman, Matthew. "Critical Thinking—What Can It Be?" *Educational Leadership*, v46 n1 Sep 1988. pp. 38-43 [EJ376244]

If schools are to succeed in teaching critical thinking, educators must have a clear idea of what it is. Critical thinking is skillful, responsible thinking that relies upon criteria, is self-correcting, and is sensitive to context.

Matthews, Dorothy, Ed. "On Teaching Critical Thinking. Cognitive Strategies for Teaching: Poetry, Short Story, Composition, the Research Paper, Critical Reading." *Illinois English Bulletin,* Illinois Association of Teachers of English, Urbana. v73 n3 Spr 1986. 75 pp. [ED267447]

Exploring a variety of ways to train students to think critically within the context of writing and literature classes, this journal issue presents cognitive strategies for teaching poetry, short stories, composition, the research paper, and critical reading.

Miller, Douglas E. "Cooperative Critical Thinking and History." *Social Studies Review,* v28 n3 Spr 1989. pp. 55-68 [EJ394346]

Argues that current social studies textbooks lack coherent formats, decipherable vocabulary, clearly written paragraphs, and presume background information which students lack. Presents a lesson which combines information from research in reading and cooperative learning techniques in an attempt to encourage discussion of information and eventual consensus in a group setting.

Morgan, Mary; Shermis, Michael. *Critical Thinking, Reading, and Writing.* Teaching Resources in the ERIC Database (TRIED) Series. [ED314728]

This book focuses on practical suggestions for developing critical thinking, reading, and writing skills at both the elementary and the secondary level. Following an introduction and a user's guide, an activities chart indicates the skills emphasized in each lesson, as well as the types of activities (such as collaborative writing, role-playing, group presentations, etc.) found in each lesson. The next section offers 19 lesson outlines involving critical thinking, reading, and writing at the elementary level, while the following section on secondary education also offers 19 such lessons. Each lesson includes a brief description, objectives, and procedures.

Neilsen, Allan R. *Critical Thinking and Reading: Empowering Learners To Think and Act.* Monograph on Teaching Critical Thinking Number 2. ERIC Clearinghouse on Reading and Communication Skills, Bloomington, IN; National Council of Teachers of English, Urbana, IL. 54 pp. 1989 [ED306543]

Intended for teachers, this monograph encourages educators to think critically both about critical reading and about what constitutes instruction of critical thinking in schools.

Newkirk, Thomas. *Critical Thinking and Writing: Reclaiming the Essay.* Monographs on Teaching Critical Thinking Number 3. ERIC Clearinghouse on Reading and Communication Skills, Bloomington, IN; National Council of Teachers of English, Urbana, IL. 56 pp. 1989 [ED309457]

This monograph argues that, unlike the structured, formulaic "school" essay, personal essays in the manner of Michel de Montaigne lead students to explore their connections with ideas and texts. Several strategies are described which use writing as a tool for critical thinking.

Norris, Stephen P. "Synthesis of Research on Critical Thinking." *Educational Leadership,* v42 n8 May 1985. pp. 40-45 [EJ319814]

Reviews the research literature on critical thinking, touching on the nature of and need for critical thinking and ensuing action, relevant findings of psychological research, the context of thought, issues in test construction, the diagnosis of thinking problems, and the need for research into the teaching of critical thinking.

Nugent, Susan Monroe, Ed. "Integrating Speaking Skills into the Curriculum." *The Leaflet,* v85 n1 Win 1986. New England Association of Teachers of English. 48 pp. [ED274002]

Stressing the importance of incorporating speech skills throughout the curriculum, the articles in this journal provide ideas for developing speaking skills in all subjects and at all levels.

Orlando, Lynn S.; Lucas, L. Berkley. "Workshop Proposal on the Strategies for the Development of Critical Thinking and Comprehension." Paper presented at the Meeting of the Conference on Critical Thinking (Newport News, VA, April 9-12, 1987). 24 pp. [ED283142]

Intended for use with elementary school reading and language arts teachers, this outline for inservice workshops in critical thinking organizes information on classroom strategies, curricula, and materials. Included are questionnaires, worksheets, and checklists on teaching the development of critical thinking and comprehension. The topics and activities covered include the following: (1) kinds of instructional materials; (2) components of direct instruction lessons; (3) a plan to involve teachers, staff and administrators in teaching thinking skills; (4) implementing various teaching strategies (direct instruction, modeling, questioning, discussion, guided practice); (5) identifying complex thinking processes, specific thinking skills, and objectives in specific subject and grade levels; (6) organizing lesson formats on focused thinking, integrated thinking, and learning-to-learn lessons; and (7) strategies for implementing learning and studying skills.

Parker, Walter C.; and others. "Dialectical Reasoning on Civic Issues." Paper presented at the Annual Meeting of the American Educational Research Association (Washington, DC, April 20-24, 1987). 42 pp. [ED281206]

Twenty-four eleventh grade students attending a month-long, summer civic-leadership institute participated in a study that examined their dialectical reasoning on civic issues. This reasoning was elicited through written scaffolding, with students guided explicitly to compose essays arguing for or against a position on a given issue. The essays were organized so that the second and third paragraphs were related dialectically, while the first and fourth were a knowledge summary and conclusion, respectively. Scaffolding within paragraphs was less explicit. The essays were analyzed to discover use of six categories of dialectical reasoning: value claims, lines of support, relevant counterarguments, empathic counterarguments, lines of counterargument, and dialectical conclusions. Results indicated (1) that most students argued both for and against their position, (2) that most summarized what they knew about the issue without apparent interference from their own bias about it, (3) that most used only one line of reasoning, (4) that most wrote an empathic paragraph about the other side of the issue, (5) that most argued against their position using just one line of reasoning, and (6) that most did not show even incipient dialectical reasoning in the concluding paragraph.

Porter, James E. "De(con)fining English: Literature, Composition, Textuality." *Journal of Teaching Writing*, v5 n1 Spr 1986. pp. 121-31 [EJ359180]

Addresses the debate over writing instruction based on canonical literature, content, great ideas, and literary theory and the debate stressing the writing process and social science based models of teaching and learning. Proposes an integrated reading and writing program emphasizing textuality—the way meaning is produced in a text by the interaction of language, audience, aim, and genre.

Ratekin, Ned; and others. "Why Teachers Resist Content Reading Instruction." *Journal of Reading*, v28 n5 Feb 1985. pp. 432-37 [EJ311431]

This article addresses the question: If content area teachers are not implementing the methods that reading educators suggest, what are the characteristics of existing instruction?

Reilly, Jamie S. "A HOT Approach to Literature in Kindergarten— Avoid the Duping of Young Minds (In the Classroom)." *Reading Teacher*, v43 n1 Oct 1989. 93 pp. [EJ396381]

Describes a literature-based activity designed to engage elementary level students in higher-order thinking skills.

Reinking, David. "Integrating Graphic Aids into Content Area Instruction: The Graphic Information Lesson." *Journal of Reading*, v30 n2 Nov 1986. pp. 146-51 [EJ342486]

Considers the use of graphic aids with regard to readers' ability to integrate graphic with written information. Points out students' need for instructional activities that develop skills such as inference through information coordination of the graphic aid, text, and prior knowledge. Presents the three stages of the GIL.

Rogers, Theresa. "Exploring a Socio-Cognitive Perspective on the Interpretive Processes of Junior High School Students." *English Quarterly,* v20 n3 Fall 1987. pp. 218-30 [EJ365840]

Discusses a study exploring the effect of the social context of two contrasting types of discussion—question and answer, and response centered—on students' interpretation of a literary work. Concludes that certain characteristics of the question and answer discussion may have inhibited students' interpretive responses.

Rowen, Anna. "Developing Critical Thinking Skills with the Newspaper." *Georgia Social Science Journal,* v21 n1 Spr 1990. pp. 22-23 [EJ411117]

Discusses the importance of newspapers in developing critical thinking skills. Presents activities from "Knowledge in Bloom," a resource guide sponsored by Newspapers in Education with learning activities keyed to Bloom's Taxonomy of Educational Objectives. Focuses on controversial issues, analyzing points of view, and using students as newspaper writers and editors.

Sacco, Steven J. "Crap Detecting: An Approach to Developing Critical Reading and Thinking Skills in the Foreign Language Curriculum." *Foreign Language Annals,* v20 n1 Feb 1987. pp. 57-66 [EJ350994]

Presents a three-part approach for developing critical reading and critical thinking skills in the foreign language curriculum. This approach seeks to (1) establish a conducive environment for critical thought; (2) sharpen students' critical eye through extensive analytical reading; and (3) sensitize students to language and language use.

Siegel, Marjorie; Carey, Robert F. *Critical Thinking: A Semiotic Perspective.* Monographs on Teaching Critical Thinking Number 1. ERIC Clearinghouse on Reading and Communication Skills, Bloomington, IN.; National Council of Teachers of English, Urbana, IL. 55 pp. 1989 [ED 303802]

This monograph for teachers encourages readers to consider the notion that thinking critically is a matter of reading signs, and that it is the functions of signs that make reflective thinking possible.

Slavin, Robert E. "Cooperative Learning and the Cooperative School." *Educational Leadership,* v45 n3 Nov 1987. pp. 7-13 [EJ367350]

Cooperative learning focuses group activity on preparing all members to succeed on individual assessments. Research findings show significantly greater achievement for the cooperatively taught class. Describes the elements of two comprehensive cooperative methods and proposes a model of a cooperative elementary school.

Smagorinsky, Peter. "Small Groups: A New Dimension in Learning." *English Journal,* v78 n2 Feb 1989. pp. 67-70 [EJ386852]

Suggests the following small group activities for improving reading comprehension: (1) introductory activities; (2) studying symbolic episodes; (3) synthesizing ideas within a literary unit; and (4) weaning students from teacher dependence.

Smith, Maggy; Salome, Peggy. "Poetry as a Springboard to Critical Thinking." *Exercise Exchange,* v35 n1 Fall 1989. pp. 36-38 [EJ394969]

Presents an assignment in which students use their study of poetry to think critically and write creatively. Describes how students synthesize inferences about a poem to write character monologs.

Smith, Carl B. "Prompting Critical Thinking." (ERIC/RCS). *Reading Teacher,* v42 n6 Feb 1989. p. 424 [EJ383731]

Discusses how teachers can provide classroom experiences that lead young readers to react critically to what they read. Offers ways to focus attention and target evaluative responses to literature.

Sorenson, Margo. "Television: Developing the Critical Viewer and Writer." *English Journal*, v78 n8 Dec 1989. pp. 42-46 [EJ403623]

Describes a three-week unit, "Television Communication and Critical Thinking," designed to make junior high students more forceful writers and discriminating viewers. Argues that by analyzing television advertising, news, and programming, students learn to think more critically about communication techniques and to use those techniques responsibly in their own writing.

Sternberg, Robert J. "Teaching Critical Thinking, Part 1: Are We Making Critical Mistakes?" *Phi Delta Kappan*, v67 n3 Nov 1985. pp. 194-98 [EJ327970]

The first part of a two-part article describes the significant differences between the kinds of problems that adults really face and the problems that students are taught to resolve in critical thinking programs.

Stotsky, Sandra. "Imagination, Writing, and the Integration of Knowledge in the Middle Grades." *Journal of Teaching Writing*, v3 n2 Fall 1984. pp. 157-90 [EJ313470]

Discusses the teaching of imaginative writing in the content area at the middle school level and indicates potential applications for such teaching at all levels. Contains extensive writing examples.

Whitmer, Jean E. "Newspaper Humor: Tool for Critical Thinking and Reading Abilities." Paper presented at the Western Humor and Irony Conference (Tempe, AZ, March 28-31, 1986). 11 pp. [ED266433]

This paper focuses on using humor to develop students' critical thinking and reading abilities. The paper suggests many newspaper humor activities for predicting word meanings through context clues, including the meanings of words in isolation and in context, in headlines, and in the comics. Next, the paper lists activities that teach inferencing with "W" and "H" questions (What? Why? When? Where? Who? and How?). The paper concludes with activities that show how newspaper humor can be developed as a tool for critical analysis of facts, opinions, and propaganda.

Williamson, Ronald; Osborne, Debra C. *Using Conceptual Analysis in the Classroom: A Writing Process Approach.* 16 pp. 1988 [ED292119]

At a time when many public school teachers and administrators are limiting instructional goals to the lower level objectives found on standardized tests, there is a need for classroom activities derived from higher purposes. Conceptual analysis, which relates abstract concepts to the lives of students, meets this need. While focusing primarily on the composing process, the technique also encourages the use of cooperative learning strategies, critical thinking skills, and interdisciplinary teaming situations. When conducting an analysis of a specified concept, students write six "cases," or stories which exemplify the concept, but without using the concept or term in question. As students compose the cases, they list related terms which are later used to form a definition of the concept. Finally, the stories are published, and a presentation is prepared which applies the concept to an issue in the everyday lives of the students.

Wolff, Mary Anne. "According to Whom? Helping Students Analyze Contrasting Views of Reality." *Educational Leadership,* v44 n2 Oct 1986. pp. 36-41 [EJ342530]

Recommends the frame of reference method in helping students learn to recognize bias in the questions an author asks, the evidence gathered, and the conclusions drawn. Describes a high school writing-anthropology unit on the Kung San society. Discusses the potentials, problems, and school-linked constraints in using frame of reference models.